Also by Jonathan Nicholas:

Hospital Beat

Kibbutz Virgin

The Tragic Romance of Africa

Oz – A Hitchhiker's Australian Anthology

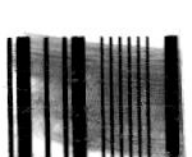

WHO'D BE A COPPER?

THIRTY YEARS A FRONTLINE BRITISH COP

JONATHAN NICHOLAS

Matador
9 Priory Business Park
Kibworth Beauchamp
Leicestershire LE8 0RX, UK
Tel: (+44) 116 279 2299
Fax: (+44) 116 279 2277
Email: books@troubador.co.uk
Web: www.troubador.co.uk/matador

ISBN 978 1784622 541

British Library Cataloguing in Publication Data.
A catalogue record for this book is available from the British Library.

Printed and bound in the UK by TJ International, Padstow, Cornwall
Typeset in Aldine by Troubador Publishing Ltd

Matador is an imprint of Troubador Publishing Ltd

To my wife, Alyson
For tolerating me.

This is a true story

Some names and identities have been changed, omitted, or disguised for legal reasons and in order to protect privacy. Otherwise, it all happened exactly as described.

'How many fingers, Winston?'

'Four! Stop it, stop it! How can you go on? Four! Four!'

'How many fingers, Winston?'

'Five! Five! Five!'

'No, Winston, that is no use. You are lying. You still think there are four. How many fingers, please?'

'Four! Five! Four! Anything you like. Only stop it, stop the pain!'

From George Orwell's
Nineteen Eighty-Four

CONTENTS

PREFACE

I recently completed thirty years as a constable in the British police. I had a very interesting time as you might expect and saw everything from petty theft to gruesome murders. But it wasn't all about crime; in fact a huge amount of time was taken up with social work, and still is today. When I joined 'the job' as it is known, it seemed the police were barely accountable to anyone. Some prisoners were often left hand-cuffed to radiators in corridors of police stations all weekend and even then when released they'd say 'Thank you' as they left. This worked pretty well in summer but in winter those old radiators were bloody hot, and the poor unfortunate scallywag would often admit anything after being partially cooked for seventy-two hours.

I worked the front line wearing a uniform in an inner city area for all of those thirty years. Not ten years, or twenty years, but three long decades. It wasn't some sleepy rural backwater either, but one of the most challenging areas of England, in a city with one of the highest crime rates in the UK. Like many British cities Nottingham has become known as a 'multi-cultural' city. But what does this really mean? How much do you really know about the Sikh way of life, the Jews living down your street, or the Muslim family who run your corner shop?

The closest thing to rural policing I ever experienced was The Forest, an incongruous bit of flat grassy area with a slope on one side in the middle of Nottingham where they usually accommodate the annual Goose Fair. There hasn't been any poaching or cattle rustling, but there have been plenty of occasions when people wandered around with illegal firearms.

I started as a foot beat officer, as everyone did in those days, in February 1984. The miners' dispute began just after this and I suddenly felt as though I'd been drafted into the army. In fact during the dispute we were often referred to as 'troops' by senior officers, which led the media to suspect that soldiers had been employed to assist in the eventual breaking of the strike. The greatest memories I have of the dispute, apart from filling in all the lucrative overtime forms, is of being continually shouted at and verbally abused all day, every day, and that was just by my colleagues. The seemingly endless boredom was occasionally punctuated by some very bland packed lunches in flimsy white cardboard boxes, the best parts of which were an apple and a Mars bar. The very long days were usually spent with a dozen other hairy-arsed coppers crammed inside a Ford Transit van inevitably exposed to copious amounts of disgusting belching and farting. There didn't seem to be any lady cops working the dispute, maybe because most ladies clearly didn't possess the necessary hairy bottoms.

After a couple of years walking the beat and almost losing my job for never actually prosecuting anyone, I was sent on a driving course. I then spent the next ten years driving 'response' cars around the city. Working as a response officer means you are usually the first on the scene at almost everything that comes in, day and night, and frequently alone. For me, and for most cops, it is a very rapid apprenticeship. I was told: "If you can do the job here, you can do it anywhere." It was certainly never boring.

In those days we didn't have any sirens in the police cars; I think they were deemed to be 'too American'. As a consequence I frequently drove a small Ford Escort at 80 mph on the wrong side of the road in built up areas in a ridiculously dangerous manner, taking both hands off the steering wheel in order to alternately press the horn, change gear, and flash the headlights, while screaming at people to get out of the way. Steering with your knees at high speed while dodging startled pedestrians is not ideal, but this was expected. Such things were done in order to 'make the job work', bending the rules to varying degrees for the sake of expediency. One of my first sergeants told me, "If you have to break the rules, don't worry, you're acting in the interests of justice."

It was known that at least unofficially you were supported and backed all the way. This and other things we did as calculated risks so the job was done as quickly as possible. Today things are very different.

I was enjoying my job and it was very exciting. I was a young man tearing around the city every day in a police car. I worked extremely hard for a long time and I didn't look up until I had a dozen years' service. When I looked around I realised just what an idiot I'd been for being so conscientious. Other cops were getting paid the same as me or more and were actually getting away with half the work. Some thoroughly bone idle colleagues also ended up acquiring quite high rank in the police service, so you clearly didn't always need to work hard to be promoted. It seemed that passing an exam and some impressive use of management clichés in interviews was all it took for some people. You'd see them every few years when you visited headquarters, but they would be another rank higher than when you last saw them, careerist cops who'd never worked shifts or undertaken any proper police work. When you've been in the job long enough you know the true nature of quite a few high ranking officers, and you remember clearly just how idle they were when they were constables.

It was not in my nature to expend endless amounts of energy avoiding work. This was how I saw it; it was quicker and easier to volunteer and just get the job done than otherwise. Not only this, a good reputation as a hard working officer would stand me in good stead, or so I thought. This naïve idea was to be proved wrong much later in my service when I had some very hurtful wrangles with the PSD, the Professional Standards Department. If you can imagine a huge and rapidly expanding department within any organisation whose main raison d'etre seems to be to unnecessarily persecute all hard working conscientious cops then this is the modern day PSD. It's the same in every UK police force nowadays. They are a bastard cross between the Soviet Stasi and the German Gestapo, but thankfully nowhere near as well-organised, professional or efficient. They seem to exist only to further their own ends, to create a climate of fear in the workplace, and to counter their own extreme paranoia. They usually operate in pairs and luckily many of them conduct themselves more like Bungle and Zippy from the children's TV show *Rainbow*. But they have the power to destroy people, and they seem to relish it.

I spent some time in the divisional control room before these were regrettably closed during one of the first rounds of disastrous budget cuts. I spent some time attached to a burglary team but still in uniform, and this was very rewarding. I've visited the scene of thousands of dwelling burglaries and witnessed the distress they cause. Burglaries are not committed by the starving but by scruffy thieving bastards who want what you've got but they are not prepared to work for it.

My last decade in the job has seen the best of times, and the very worst. I spent most of this looking after an inner city hospital, thoroughly enjoying myself. I acquired close to £30,000 in grant funding from various sources to help the kids on the nearby council estate stay away from crime and antisocial behaviour with my music club project. I achieved some great results too, and was awarded the title of 'Community Police Officer of the Year' in 2007. The first half of my service saw a huge investment in the British police service, and latterly I've witnessed the wholesale dismantling of that same great service. If it is destroyed much more then there is a real danger it will be lost forever. I can say this because I've seen it; I've worked at the sharp end for thirty years.

Sadly all my energies in the last few years of my service seemed to have been spent defending myself against my own employers rather than doing my job. I was not alone. Many of my honest, hard working colleagues in the police felt the wrath of the PSD. I know one colleague who was suspended on full pay for *three and a half years* before finally being completely exonerated. Taxpayers kept him at home on full pay all that time, when he could have been at work. I know this might sound bizarre but it's true, and it's very common nowadays. It seems that a hugely disproportionate amount of time, money and effort is spent by police forces across the country investigating their own employees rather than safeguarding the public from child killers, thieves and other scum that continue to wander our streets with impunity.

People I meet in the pub frequently bemoan having to

work in a job they hate until their late sixties, and see me with envious eyes drawing a generous public sector pension. But I am one of the last, an endangered species, a cop who has actually reached retirement age. Perhaps I should be stuffed and mounted in the British Museum? It is my prediction that very few people in the police service will achieve this in the future, mainly because they will add ten years to the pensionable service, but if the PSD don't get you then the draconian sickness policy will. You will either find yourself in prison for making a genuine mistake or sacked for stupidly getting yourself injured on duty while perhaps trying to save someone's life.

Books about the police and the wider public sector sell really well, even the very poor ones that clearly haven't been properly proof-read or copy-edited, and particularly those written from the inside. Such books are quite rare because according to the Home Office and ACPO (Association of Chief Police Officers) serving police officers should not write about their job. Those who do are clearly taking a risk, and many are therefore written anonymously. Even so, they have to keep their scribblings innocent, amusing, vague and inoffensive. I can write what I like, even if it brings the police service into disrepute, because I don't work for them anymore. So, make yourself a mug of coffee, sit back and enjoy the ride.

Jonathan Nicholas, October 2014

JOINING

RETURNING FROM ABROAD

How did I evolve from a long-haired, tree-hugging hippy to become one of 'Thatcher's bully boys'? The process was gradual, involving months of training and a good deal of introspection on my part. Everyone has the freedom to choose their own lifestyle, either to follow a dream, however realistic or ridiculous, or to drift along aimlessly, for years or even their entire life. We all face career decisions of one sort or another when young, and I chose to join the police service, though I'm not entirely sure why. I vaguely remember my father saying something about a good pension, but this never occurred to me when I joined. You don't think of such boring things when you are in your early twenties. In the latter days of my service my pension was costing me a small fortune in compulsory contributions, a fact that is not widely known.

I didn't give much serious thought to becoming a cop, or anything else for that matter, though I did have a few vague ideas. I had my share of drifting; from the age of eighteen to twenty-three, when I wandered the globe as a scruffy vagrant traveller, wide-eyed and fantastically naïve, moving from one country to another, my passport folded over in my back pocket. That wonderful document was quite often the only thing I ever possessed. It was all I needed, my ticket to freedom.

I was looking for something positive to do with my life,

seeking a reason for it all. This probably sounds like complete and utter nonsense but it's true. Some people like me develop late and have obscure ideas about what they want to do. In my case these ideas were often muddled by cheap alcohol and drugs, while slumped in some desert *wadi* or lying on an endless Australian beach.

I'd been bumbling along since I was eighteen, drifting around the world living a stateless, bohemian lifestyle until I reached the age of twenty-three. Then quite suddenly on a fine New Zealand autumn morning in April 1983 I ran out of inspiration. At that moment while sitting on the clean white sand of Auckland's North Shore I felt ready to return to the UK and find a career. It wasn't a kind of epiphany, but more likely a rare moment of clarity caused by not being drunk or bombed off my tits on weed for almost three months. For years I'd lived with no money and no belongings except for a diary, a rucksack and a change of clothes. But I was incredibly happy. I didn't own anything, but I was free. This was to be the sort of priceless, wonderful freedom I was about to willingly give up for the next thirty years.

My parents were noticeably much older when I saw them again for the first time in years at Heathrow airport. They appeared frail, and this lent some urgency to my situation, as their apparent leap in years made me feel older too. It was good to be back in the UK, but this time I knew I was here to stay. No more brief stops before flying off again to some other exotic hiding place. This was finally the end. The wandering had to stop. But what should I do? I felt like Richard Hannay returning from South Africa in John Buchan's *The Thirty Nine Steps*. I was home and yet I needed something exciting and interesting to keep me in England.

I lay on a bedroom floor in my parent's bungalow listening to music, staring idly at the ceiling, occasionally turning my head to watch the heavy rain running in tiny riverlets on the window. I watched them compete with one another as they raced down the glass, always an unseen outsider leaping ahead to beat my favourites.

I had been allocated a bed, but preferred the floor, like *Crocodile Dundee* in his plush New York hotel room; I'd been so used to sleeping on the ground in my vagrant lifestyle that I found a soft bed quite uncomfortable. This was a habit that remained with me for years. The dismal view from the window matched my mood. It was entirely grey, with the tops of nearby trees in spring bud held back, jostling one another constantly in a strong north wind. The sun was gone, and blue sky was nowhere to be seen as though banished into memory. It was a typically cold English spring day; damp, miserable and claustrophobic. The dark clouds covered the ground like a fire blanket, blotting out light as though a hundred miles thick. I was in a place where there were no sun-drenched beaches and blood-warm ocean. Life seemed incredibly vacuous and dull, and I wondered where I'd left my passport.

My brother-in-law Malcolm arrived at the house. My bedroom door was slightly ajar and I could just see him as he stomped in through the front door. He brushed the rain from his sleeves, and I noticed his thick glasses and moustache were speckled with raindrops. I knew the purpose of his visit. He'd brought with him an application form for the police, for me. I'd applied for other jobs, but had not thought about a career in the police. Surely I couldn't entertain such an idea? How would I cope with the rigours of a disciplined organisation? I'd been living a carefree existence for so long, how would I fit into such a way of life? Would I be able to?

I'd been an air cadet for years as a teenager, and thoroughly enjoyed it. I'd reached the rank of flight sergeant. Life in a disciplined organisation would not be *entirely* alien, but for the last few years I'd been such a free agent, completely at liberty to do anything I wanted.

Malcolm stepped into the room and handed me the papers.

"Just fill it in and see how you go. If you get in, you wouldn't have to stay. Try it. If you don't like it, you could always leave. You wouldn't be tied in, not like the forces."

I was still lying on the floor listening to music. I knew Malcolm was trying to help, so I nodded, probably too casually, and smiled. I sat up and leaned against the bed. Malcolm was a special constable at the time, a volunteer police officer, and he'd picked up the form from the local police station. He disappeared away into the kitchen. I heard him talk to my mother. I sensed that I was the topic of conversation because they glanced in my direction, talking in hushed conspiratorial tones. I heard my mother's voice.

"Is he up yet?" But I didn't hear Malcolm's reply. I'd been home a few months and I still didn't feel right. I took solace in a friend's company and we smoked hash occasionally, but I knew this was the wrong thing to do. I was evading the truth and I couldn't hide forever. The Genesis song *Mama* was high in the charts at the time, and even now it reminds me of those days, with the guilt of it all tearing me apart.

I think everyone in the family, including myself, were disappointed that my great wanderings hadn't amounted to much. I'd returned from years of travelling abroad to absolutely nothing, apart from a stack of sun-bleached and very tattered travel diaries. But what good were these? I didn't have any money, and I wasn't any further qualified in anything than when I left. But I'd experienced hardship in many forms, not infrequent and lengthy spells of hunger, some danger, and times of heartache and desperation. I hadn't realised that when you experience real hunger your teeth begin to feel quite erroneous in the mouth, and actually start to hurt, very gradually along with everything else. I'd been very hungry in Athens, and again ten thousand miles away in Darwin. I'd loved and lost; I'd seen some amazing things and had a great adventure. Perhaps more than anything else I had gained a quiet determination to succeed and a self-reliance that would remain with me for the rest of my life.

I scanned the very comprehensive application form. There were twenty or more pages, and it appeared to be a research paper for an edition of *This is your Life*, with me being the subject matter. Starting from birth to the present day I was asked to supply details of *every* address I'd ever lived at, every job, and all incidents which I thought my prospective employers might need to know about. How honest should I be? I'd lived in Australia for a year as an illegal immigrant when my tourist visa expired. I'd shared a flat in Brisbane with a chap whose brother was a drug dealer on the Gold Coast, and we were two of his best customers. Should I tell them? Would they find out?

Should I tell them about the many occasions I sneaked under the fence into Gaza city in 1980 avoiding the Israeli checkpoints to smoke hash with Palestinians on the beach? What about my time in Germany as a labourer when I shared a damp tenement with some Irish and Polish guys? There were times the German police visited us in their smart green uniforms after reports of drunkenness in our slum house, clearly evident to our complaining neighbours. What, if anything, should I tell them about that?

I decided I'd merely list the addresses, and leave it to them as to how far they would check my past activities. If they found out everything and turned me down as a result, then so be it. Thankfully I'd never been arrested anywhere in the world, and never came to police notice, apart from a few minor encounters. On one occasion two Australian cops checked me out when I was hitch-hiking. I was standing alone by a melting road which stretched to the end of the earth, hoping for a lift out of Katherine, south of Darwin. A small group of Aborigines were gathered together in the scant shade of a ghost gum tree near the road and I was contemplating joining them. As usual I was broke, hungry and thirsty. The cops spoke to me in a very business-like, if slightly racist manner, checking my identity and my intentions, before telling me to: "Stay away from the Abbos, mate!"

Another occurred when I was almost caught climbing the Storey Bridge high above the Brisbane River. Almost. The rotten Greek police once ripped open my toothpaste and my last bit of soap at Athens airport, just because I had long hair down my back, a filthy unkempt beard, tatty clothes, and a generally malodorous whiff about me.

I was later to find out that during my application process there had been some extensive background checks made on my activities. In the UK, police forces in Derbyshire, Lincolnshire, Norfolk and South Yorkshire were consulted. The Australian police in Queensland visited at least one address I had given on the application form. Two of Joe Bjelke-Petersen's finest male uniformed cops called in at an address in Coorparoo, a suburb of Brisbane where I'd lived for a while. An old friend remembered me and confirmed I'd lived there. It was a good job the cops didn't attend a few weeks later, when the address was raided and my friend was busted for growing a ton of weed in the back garden. Police were also consulted in Jerusalem, but luckily, like all the other places I'd lived in, I'd never been tangled up with the local law.

For much of the time when I was travelling my hair and beard were very long, so I have to admit I probably did appear to look like precisely what I was: a scruffy, unwashed vagrant, similar to the tattered soul scrambling up the beach at the start of every *Monty Python* TV show. I had become quite wary of authority, and viewed the police – all police – with a mixture of suspicion, fear and, at the very least, indifference. Overall, they were to be avoided.

A POLICEMAN CALLS

I filled in the application form in the early summer of 1983 with a degree of casual indifference and sent it off. I hoped it would be the last such repetitive police paperwork I would ever have to spend time on. Sadly of course, it was a sign of things to come.

I heard nothing for quite some time. Then I received a letter briefly acknowledging my application and stating someone would phone in order to arrange a convenient time to visit me at home. Sure enough, a few days later, on a typically blustery June afternoon the doorbell rang and a very tall male officer in his late twenties stood at the door to my parents' bungalow in full uniform. He had a thin, angular face, and he was wearing a long black greatcoat, unbuttoned, but no headgear. I assumed he'd parked a vehicle nearby. A blue *Burndept* radio was slung around his neck inside his tunic, and faint electronic voices chattered occasionally. He introduced himself and I ushered him in. He moved slowly and deliberately like a young Jimmy Stewart and sat rather stiffly on the edge of the sofa. His immaculate black boots looked incongruous on the carpet, and the toe caps shone like glass as though he'd just been on parade. He looked around the room as he spoke, scanning the house and décor.

"So, you want to join the police then?" he said, rather obviously, smiling at me. He then scowled a little, as if making an assessment of me and looking for some reaction. I guessed I should make some form of positive reply so I offered:

"Yes. I think so. It's a good job, isn't it?" I said, feeling rather stupid. He seemed very polite; unlike the officious German, rude Greek, and brusque, business-like Australian police I'd encountered in the past. I could only half believe I was trying to become one of them, a member of the establishment, having lived on the other side for years.

"Yes, it is. It's not all excitement though. There's a lot of other stuff, boring stuff, things you don't see on the telly." He looked serious and distracted. His radio seemed to be a constant source of irritation, and he tilted his head slightly to one side as though trying to listen to it, like a bird seeking a worm, while talking to me at the same time.

"Yes, I know. It's not all like *The Sweeney*, is it?" and I laughed a little, trying to lighten the encounter. He didn't seem impressed. I remembered the first inklings I'd had of possibly wanting to join the police, years before, sitting in the churchy gloom of a packed television room at Kibbutz Dafna in northern Israel, crowding in with everyone else to watch *The Sweeney* in grainy black and white.

"No. We deal with the same families time and again. It runs in the generations."

I hadn't a clue what he was talking about. What runs in the generations? He fiddled with his radio, adjusting the volume slightly, turning a knob at the side without looking at it. I wondered how he knew which way it was turned. He spoke into it briefly, pressing the small yellow transmit button on the top, as though in response to a request, which I didn't hear, then turned his attention to me.

"How did you know they wanted you, just then?" I

asked, genuinely curious. I could hardly hear anything legible from the walkie-talkie around his neck, let alone a name of any sort.

"They just shouted my collar number, see?" and he touched the series of shiny metallic numbers on his right shoulder. He smiled at me. "You get used to it."

I made us both a cup of tea and he gulped his incredibly quickly as though his throat was lined with asbestos. I spoke about my vague knowledge of the police, which amounted to information gained from watching TV shows such as *The Sweeney, Starsky and Hutch, Kojak* and so on. I even had recollections of much older programmes like *Z-Cars* and *Softly Softly*. I remember Bert Lynch, the sergeant in *Z-Cars* standing at a sink shaving in the afternoon. As a child I remember thinking how unusual this seemed because my dad always shaved early in the morning.

I told the policeman about my Uncle Alan who at the time was a detective sergeant in West Yorkshire police. Alan always had a world-weary rudeness about him; a tired knowingness that I now understand had grown from years of repeatedly dealing with society's worst human detritus. I'd heard him speaking to my dad using words like 'cunt' and 'fuck' in conversation, which clearly embarrassed my father. I'd never once heard my own father use such language.

This was the only direct connection I had with the job at the time, apart from the fact that my dad actually seemed more than a little anti-police. He'd based his poor opinions of police officers on some dreadful experiences in South Africa in the 1950s, hardly relevant to modern Britain.

I briefly mentioned some of my travels to the young cop, but he couldn't have seemed less interested, so I didn't raise it again. I remember he told me he'd been to France on a school trip, which was the sum total of his travel experience. I am always slightly bemused when people tell me they've never been abroad, or have never owned a passport. Travel has been such a formative part of my life. Even so, I don't readily discuss my experiences so the absence of them in someone else's life is not a huge issue for me.

I heard a barely audible but peremptory female voice on the cop's radio and he responded.

"Yes. Ten four. I'm not far away. I'll attend that now." He sounded as though he worked for the LAPD rather than a British police force. Nottinghamshire still used 'Ten Codes' radio abbreviations at the time.

"I'll have to go. Thanks for the tea. You should hear from us soon." He stood up and handed me his empty mug. He thrust his right hand at me and I instinctively took it. We shook hands firmly for a few moments. He smiled at me in a manner that I couldn't help thinking was as though he felt sorry for me. I showed him the door; he stepped out and disappeared down the driveway, his long black coat flapping behind him like a cape. It had just started raining heavily. I had no idea as to the real purpose of his visit. He didn't write anything down. It has occurred to me now as I write this, that my visitor has probably long since retired, now a big fat bloke who spends all his spare time tending to his pigeons and supping ale at his local pub. Good on him I say; I've reached that point myself, except for the pigeons. Other than that he's probably dead, poor chap. One of the least desirable police traditions is that many cops die quite soon after retirement.

More time passed. Weeks in fact. I occupied myself as I had the previous few months; reading and writing in my diary. I have always kept a diary, and always will. If you've ever met me – even briefly – then I'm afraid I've probably written reams about you. I write in it every day, even if it's just a few lines. I read Graham Chapman's hilarious book *A Liar's Autobiography*. I read George Orwell's *Down and out in Paris and London,* which I could thoroughly relate to, and his book about the English, *The Lion and the Unicorn.* He stated in this book that the British would never allow fascists to march the goose step on British streets, because we would just laugh at them. I'm not sure this applies any more. I read Miles Kington's book *Miles and Miles*, and *Creator* by Jeremy Leven. An interesting read, even though a lot of it was just pornographic twoddle. Such similar twoddle that now sells millions of copies.

I also read Orwell's *Nineteen Eighty Four*, which I found incredibly claustrophobic and disturbing, but brilliant nonetheless. The total distortion of truth by Big Brother, in a world where cameras watch our every move and the government tells us what we can and can't say. I remember lying on my bedroom floor reading it in one day, only venturing out to use the toilet every few hours, the rain still lashing down heavily against the window. The movie version starring John Hurt and Richard Burton in his last film role before his untimely death was also superb.

Finally in early August I was summoned to attend a huge building in the centre of Nottingham adjacent to the main fire station, known as Central Police Station. It was only the second time in my life I'd been to Nottingham.

Central Police Station was a purpose-built grey brick building with wide staircases and carved stone lions sitting proudly atop sweeping curved bannisters. It was an imposing building constructed in the 1930s and it was in one of the front ground floor offices that I sat the standard entrance exam. This was a straightforward arithmetic and English test which I was relieved to find was quite easy. Various out-of-date recruitment posters hung limply on the walls, clinging on with faded sticky tape, as though placed there years before as a perfunctory gesture. The rooms were dark and smelt of polished wood, layers of dust and stale tobacco, like a cheap Spanish hotel.

I was subjected to a very basic medical examination, with the usual coughing and holding of testicles routine conducted by a man who I presumed was a doctor, though I don't remember him telling me who he was. There aren't many men who've had my balls in their hands, and luckily his were very warm. I was weighed while just wearing underpants (eleven stone twelve pounds) and my height checked. I'd put on quite a bit of weight since my travels came to an end. I was an emaciated ten stone (a hundred and forty pounds) when I returned from travelling a few months before. Food was never a priority for me, and I would frequently substitute a few fags for a meal, in common with many ardent smokers. I was just short of six feet tall, without shoes.

I was interviewed briefly by a red-faced and corpulent uniformed sergeant who had an easy-going manner. I sensed by his age and demeanour that he was probably close to retirement and as such didn't really care anymore. I was told before I left that I'd passed the day's proceedings and I was on to the next stage.

In September I was visited by another cop from the local station in Retford. The sergeant was approaching middle age, probably late forties, and he looked weary and distracted. He seemed relieved when I offered him a cup of tea, and he fell heavily onto the sofa in the lounge as though he planned to stay for the rest of his life. He sighed, smiled and then asked questions about my family. He took out a yellow *Bic* biro and a sheet of A4 paper which he folded over twice and rested on one knee. I didn't know it at the time but his job was to complete a 'Home Surroundings Report', something the young constable had apparently initiated weeks before. He seemed more interested in my dad's greenhouse, visible from the window and now packed with ripe tomatoes in final flourish. He asked me if I undertook any of the gardening, and he was clearly disappointed when I said no. He didn't seem to allow his radio to bother him to the extent the constable did.

He finally left after two large mugs of sweet tea, half a packet of digestive biscuits and a tour of my parents' garden. As he walked away I noticed the leaves on the trees above the nearby lane had just started to curl a little at the edges. What little summer we had that year was in full retreat and I noticed a cool autumnal chill in the air. My first winter in years was rapidly approaching.

WAITING

For the purposes of researching this book, I took a formal look at my official personal record several times. I say 'official' because there is clearly an official and an unofficial personal record kept of every police officer, though this is denied. I was once at Central Police Station years ago and blundered almost by chance into the Personnel Office. There were neat rows of files on open shelves and I clearly saw my own collar number amongst the others in numerical order. I reached up to take hold of it but just before I did so, and with my hand barely a few inches away I was shouted at by a female from across the room:

"No! No! You can't! You need an appointment!" she screeched at me in a loud panic, to which I turned and replied in all innocence: "I'm here now; this is my file, surely..." The woman who was the owner of the peremptory shrieking sprang to her feet from behind a desk and quickly forced herself between me and the file, still on the shelf. She calmed down very quickly, probably aware of just how erratic she was behaving and still breathless said to me again:

"You need to give us half an hour, at least. We'll have it ready for you then, okay?"

I looked on, bemused, but returned thirty minutes later to find it laid out across a desk, neatly opened at page one and the date I had joined. I asked to see it again, just prior to retirement, and the same thing happened then too. If they have nothing to hide, as they claim, then I ask you, why would they behave in such a manner? They forget they are dealing with cops, suspicious people who deal with duplicity on a daily basis.

I managed to take a look at all the initial comments made about me on my typed application form. Someone had written on the front of the form by hand: '*Male, 23yrs, single. Much travelled – please see attached list – Jewish faith possibly.*' This observation was no doubt made as a result of some time I'd spent working on a kibbutz in Israel. It always amazes me that there is an automatic assumption of Jewishness about this. If you visit the Vatican City in Rome does this make you a Roman Catholic? Well, yes, I suppose it might, but a summer spent working in Germany didn't arouse a comment such as: '*Loves Germany – must be a Nazi – possibly*'. I usually keep people guessing, as I decided early on that my religion – like my sexual preference – was my business and no-one else's. However, my religion was listed on the comprehensive form in the bit where it says: '*Religion: C of E*', so this person was clearly making an inaccurate presumption. The visiting sergeant had written:

'The applicant is a fairly impressive looking young man of good height and build. He has a good conversational ability and has apparently mixed a very great deal with many types and nationalities. He has travelled all over the world and prides himself upon his independence.'

He made no reference to the tomatoes in my dad's greenhouse. The sergeant from Central Police Station had written:

'Did well on day's tests. Very confident with slightly familiar attitude. Mature with broad experience of life through worldwide travels. Speaks well and converses freely.'

Finally, in summing up, another sergeant had written:

'Panel felt if he could come to terms with discipline he has a lot to offer the service. His application form is one of the most comprehensive that I have seen and probably gives some insight into his character. I would recommend that he be considered for appointment.'

In the autumn of 1983 amid widespread controversy the US Air Force delivered dozens of cruise missiles in some highly visible wooden crates to RAF Greenham Common. It was the height of the Cold War, and President Ronald Reagan and Prime Minister Margaret Thatcher were constantly in the media standing together, reaffirming their determination to protect the Free World by importing ever more American nuclear weapons into Britain. I drove by the protesters' 'Peace Camp' surrounding the airbase when I visited a friend in Reading, and saw lots of well-intentioned women living rough in flimsy shelters made from plastic bags.

I was dealing with my own personal battle too: I was trying to quit smoking. It was almost five years to the day in November 1978 when I smoked my first cigarette in the factory at Kibbutz Dafna in Israel, during my first night shift on the dreaded Conveyor. But now I was determined to quit, so I bought myself some stick-on merit stars from *Woolworths* in Retford and made a chart of each long and agonising day without a smoke. It seemed to work. Those were the days before e-cigarettes and nicotine replacements. It was cold turkey and nothing else.

I ran around the village each day and went swimming at night in order to give myself some incentive to become healthy again. I was thin when I was travelling but not particularly healthy. In our very fat-conscious society today people frequently mistake being thin for being in good health, but this is simply not true. I've always run though. I used to run to school. Wherever I travelled if I was eating reasonably well, which wasn't all that often, I'd run.

Caught up in Cold War fervour while waiting to hear from the police, I joined the local branch of the Royal Observer Corps. The primary reason of course was that if the bomb dropped, as it seemed it might, I'd know where all the fallout shelters were, and I'd have ready access to them. Every week I would make my way to a secret location in the corner of a farmer's field where there was a very discreet steel hatch in the ground, standing slightly proud of a low concrete base. You'd never have guessed it was there. I'd climb thirty feet down a metal ladder to meet the other members of the team. Amid a huge stockpile of tinned food and bottled water we would play out a possible scenario which we hoped none of us would ever see.

Wherever a nuclear weapon detonated nearby, one of us would have to go up to the surface and place a sheet of radiation-absorbent card in a metal frame, and turn it towards the blast. It was unclear which of us was to do this erroneous task, as clearly whoever it was would have probably been blown to smithereens or at the very least glow in the dark for days to come. The idea was that the direction of the fallout could then be predicted, thereby forecasting where the worst of the radiation would make landfall. This information would then be passed on to the authorities using a black Bakelite telephone. The government would be safely ensconced deep underground of course, as we were, well out of harm's way.

It occurred to me that if nuclear war did happen, the government would survive perfectly intact but there'd be bugger-all left on the surface to govern, just a burning wilderness of ruined buildings and millions of dead people.

At the time of course it all seemed very logical. Nuclear Armageddon was a real possibility in those days. In reality, I suspect we would have all just brought our families into the safety of the nearest secret bunker and waited it out, while everyone else on the surface burned to a crisp. This was strongly hinted at by some of the older members of the local Corps, along with the undeniably interesting prospect of being trapped underground for weeks or months with one or two lovely looking young ladies. But even with that thought in mind, I'm very glad it remained at the theoretical stage. One of the most unrealistic elements of disaster movies with an 'end of the world' scenario is they always portray cops and other emergency services carrying out their duties right up to the end. Do you think for a moment these people would abandon their own families in such circumstances?

Finally in December 1983 I received a letter stating I was to attend a whole day of interviews and tests the following month at the local police training centre. Two days before this letter arrived, on 17th December 1983, a huge car bomb exploded outside Harrods in central London. A warning had been given and the police attended. Four Metropolitan police officers had been approaching the suspect vehicle on foot just as it exploded. They had probably been thinking about grabbing a bacon cob and a cup of tea a few moments before. Three were killed outright, and one survived but lost both his legs. Three members of the public were also killed, one of them an American citizen, visiting London for some Christmas shopping. Ninety other people were injured. The Provisional IRA later apologised for the loss of life, a rather cynical thing to do that immediately makes you wonder why it was done in the first place.

Not only was it the height of the Cold War, but the IRA

INTERVIEWS AND TESTS

EPPERSTONE MANOR

I arrived at Epperstone Manor, the beautiful but discreetly crumbling training establishment belonging to Nottinghamshire Constabulary, at 8.30am, January 6th 1984. Epperstone was a typically quiet English village which had a pub, a post office and perhaps a few dozen houses mostly strung out along the main road through the village. There were two short rows of police houses across the road from the manor, used for residential training courses.

When on a training course of more than a day or so you could live there if you wished, in that beautiful quiet village, free of charge. The manor was exactly as it sounds, an old manor house, the size of a small stately home. It was a wonderful building with beautiful views across sweeping lawns and rolling countryside. Rows of crown-topped terracotta chimney pots on the steeply sloping roofs were an indication of huge stone fireplaces in each room. There were stag's heads hanging from dark oak-panelled walls, with a wide dark wood staircase, each step of which creaked wonderfully underfoot. Huge oil paintings adorned the walls on very thick picture wire, immaculate red carpet covered all the floors and there was an almost palpable atmosphere of tradition and sense of purpose. This was the focal point of the training establishment and it evoked an immediate sense of awe and respect.

I met six other male candidates, and after a very civilized

cup of tea in delicate china cups with the force crest on each side, we were ushered into an oak-panelled room off the main hall. Desks had been laid out, carefully spaced, and we sat down. There were eight places, and seven of us, so maybe one person had changed his mind? We were handed five papers consisting of various written tests: logical reasoning, mathematics, spelling, grammar and vocabulary. There was also a current affairs paper, with questions such as 'What is Greenham Common?'

Half an hour into the tests the eighth, missing candidate arrived. He sauntered into the room, smiling rather witlessly, taking his seat in a conspicuously unhurried fashion, looking blankly around as though settling down for a picnic on the beach. I wondered how anyone so remarkably gormless could even apply for the police let alone arrive so late. I assumed that perhaps he wasn't too bothered about it. I assumed correctly because about eighteen months later he resigned.

At 10.30am we had all finished the written tests and were led out of the main doors across a small car park and around the corner towards a row of garages. Opposite these were some changing rooms and showers. We filed inside and were instructed to change into PT gear we'd brought with us from home. There followed a timed run of a mile and a half. This length was quite fortuitous as it was roughly the same distance I'd been running almost every day since I returned home in April.

We stood around waiting for the off like eager race horses, our breath clouding around us in the freezing air. Then at a gentle jog we were led past the huge wrought-iron gates by an instructor who turned right down the main street towards the village. The sky was wonderfully clear on what was a perfectly crisp January day. When I lived in Brisbane I'd occasionally long for a day such as this, just once in a while, during the long, sweltering months of summer.

I noticed permanently shaded areas of grass by the road had become thick frosted spikes and the leafless branches of the trees strained skywards like skeletal fingers, everything utterly lifeless in the middle of winter. The air was so cold it burned the back of my throat like boiling water at every breath. After a few hundred yards the PT instructor, a diminutive ginger-haired chap who clearly possessed bionic legs, turned left and started up a hill called Chapel Lane. It was very steep and known locally as Chapel Hill.

The instructor, in his sharply pressed shorts and sleeveless vest, began to draw ahead, as was no doubt expected, but I was fairly close behind him, leading the others in the group. Once we had reached the top of the hill panting furiously like a pack of hunting dogs we turned around and ran back down towards the manor. The instructor disappeared ahead and a few minutes later he was standing at the gates stop-watch in hand as we arrived. I was first to trudge into view and finished with a time of seven minutes and twenty-eight seconds, which was pretty good. I'd forced myself to such an extent that I felt quite sick. My usual time for such a distance was about ten minutes. The others returned quite spaced apart, also looking red-faced and exhausted. All members of the group completed the run in less than eleven minutes. Twelve minutes was the pass-mark.

There was a small gym area across from the changing rooms. Thick mats had been laid out across the concrete floor, next to some free weights and static equipment. We were then asked to perform a series of sit-ups, push-ups and squat jumps against the clock. I didn't have a huge amount of upper body strength at the time so I didn't do particularly well. A chap called Tony did the best out of all of us at these exercises, and seemed ultra-fit. We then had a communal shower. There was some serious talk as to what might follow. The conversations were guarded and restrained, and very formal in nature, almost as though this too was being assessed.

We returned to the classroom where we'd taken the written tests, and the chairs were now laid out in a semi-circle to the front of the room. I felt invigorated from the run so I quite enjoyed the next task. We were each asked in turn to stand up at the front and give a short unprepared talk of two minutes' duration about ourselves. It was clear that we formed quite an interesting bunch. One had just left the Royal Navy, one the Merchant Navy, university, private industry, one was already in the police as a cadet, and there was even a semi-professional footballer.

A group discussion followed, while people with clipboards watched us at the back looking shifty, jotting things down occasionally. The subject of the discussion was: 'The Greenham Common peace protesters'. I contributed where I could, and at least as much as anyone else, acutely aware that at least *some* contribution was expected. I wondered what the assessors were looking for. Everyone's opinions were safely far from extreme, and generally supportive of the government of the day. No doubt if one of us had said: "All those scruffy lefty protesters should be dragged away by the hair and shot" or even at the other end of the spectrum: "They're right to protest, nuclear weapons are wrong and so are Reagan and Thatcher and this fascist government", then there would be some conspicuous scribbling on the clipboards. I suspect we all realised this, so we made our observations very measured, polite and sensible.

I enjoyed the morning, and felt reasonably confident about my performance. Lunch in the canteen was excellent: battered fish with cheese, (always fish on a Friday – did they assume we were all Catholic?) chips and mushy peas, then apple pie and custard. As candidates, this was all supplied free of charge using meal tokens, issued to us on arrival. Tea followed, in the force liveried cups and saucers. It was all extremely civilised, and we were made to feel very special as a result. We felt honoured at the prospect of joining Nottinghamshire Constabulary, an organisation that was clearly proud of itself.

The canteen was a short walk from the manor house along a flagged path which cut through pristine lawns overlooking superb grounds. There was a bowling green, some hard tennis courts, and further down a grass bank, a rugby field and cricket pitch. At the very bottom a line of tall mature poplars marked the boundary of the extensive grounds. It really was a beautiful setting. One of the candidates, Dave, a very tall chap with a bushy moustache, offered his *Embassy Number 1s* around the table. Sadly, after several weeks' successful abstinence I relented and took one. We sat around the dining table smoking and chatting about the day. The final part was still to come: the interview.

We were called in turn into a very plush office in the manor. I was standing gazing out of the window when my name was called, my mind wandering back to my travelling days. I was also wondering who the family had been that had occupied the manor years before, and what had become of them.

I spent thirty minutes talking mainly about myself. A small, bearded, uniformed inspector listened to my rambling as he sat ensconced behind a huge, polished wood desk, his torso squeezed tightly into a crumpled white shirt. He glared at me with a wide toothy grin across his shiny face. He wasn't a bad looking bloke I suppose, with features that made him look like a cross between Stewart Granger and Roy 'Chubby' Brown. He had an air of authority that he was clearly aware of, and which gave him the demeanour of Baron Bomburst from *Chitty Chitty Bang Bang*. He was flanked on one side by a woman who was as plain as an old pit boot, which wasn't helped by her dark clothing. She did very little other than smile a lot and occasionally make brief notes. A smaller, thin man in plain clothes who I believe was also an inspector sat at the other side of the Baron. He also made notes but appeared more like one of those nodding dogs you might see on the rear parcel shelf of an old car, moving his head around to some inaudible rhythm.

They looked at me intently as I was asked about my parents, my aspirations, hopes, fears and my many previous jobs. I was asked more than once whether I would be able to handle the discipline. I reminded them of my four years in the air cadets, and how I'd become a glider pilot in record time at RAF Lindholme (now a prison) and then a private pilot of aeroplanes, which in itself requires a not insubstantial amount of self-discipline. I hoped that I came across as quietly confident, rather than cocky or arrogant.

I waited outside, and in only a few minutes the Baron bounded out of the room. He was smiling broadly and his generous belly completely obscured his belt as though he had a medicine ball under his clothing. His shirt buttons were bursting under the pressure and I could see masses of greying hair straining to reach out from his distended belly. I didn't like to tell him his shirt was hanging out on the right side like a fallen corner flag. I've no doubt he was probably a nice man, and he certainly commanded a presence, even if he did have egg stains and rice pudding globules on his tie. He gripped my hand and shook it warmly:

"You've been successful today. Your application will continue, well done. We'll be in touch for the final interview," he said, loud and confident like a miniature Brian Blessed.

FORCE HEADQUARTERS

The following Tuesday I attended a doctor's in the centre of Nottingham for a chest x-ray, followed by a final comprehensive medical examination. I was stunned at the blackness of my lungs, but I was told it wasn't bad, for a smoker, probably due to all the running. But it left a deep impression on me, and it provoked further determination to quit permanently. Dave Gilmour of Pink Floyd was prompted in a similar manner apparently, when he heard himself cough on their 1975 album *Wish You Were Here*. You can hear him clear his throat if you listen carefully at the start of the title track.

The time I spent between returning home from my travels and starting my police career was quite a dark period for me. I was ready to work hard in my new job but felt frustration as every day passed while living in a state of limbo-like penury. I found it extremely tiresome living from one dole cheque to the next. I could only imagine a whole life lived in such a way to be stifling and soul-destroying. Funds were almost always inadequate and there was little to do other than exist on a very basic level. While travelling around foreign countries this penurious condition was acceptable to me as part of the experience, but now at home I felt anxious and even a little bitter that I was effectively excluded from mainstream society, without a steady job and all the positives that come with it. This gave me a real taste of a life on benefits in Britain, and some lasting sympathy for those who are genuinely trapped in this awful lifestyle. It was now 1984 and I'd been home, and on the dole, since April the previous year.

I read more. RF Delderfield's *To Serve Them All My Days* was a lovely book, as was his novel *Diana*. I listened to a lot of music, of course. Dire Straits were in the charts with *Telegraph Road*, and my old favourite, Genesis, with further commercially successful songs in addition to *Mama*. But Genesis had changed, and I started to feel old at twenty-three, when their music began to sound overly commercial, in my humble opinion, and I longed to hear them play more music like their 1977 *Seconds Out* album. I also read Dirk Bogarde's novel *A Gentle Occupation*, which was wonderful. I continued to visit my favourite pub in Sheffield, The Hare and Hounds, but of course a lot of time had passed, and there were very few of my old friends still left who frequented the place. Our usual corner of the pub was vacant, and the emptiness screamed loudly as a stark reminder that my carefree youth was over. Then it occurred to me that it's often not a *place* that is wonderful to visit or live in, but the *people* contained within.

In the beginning of February 1984 I spent four hours at Nottinghamshire Police Headquarters. Compared to Epperstone Manor, Sherwood Lodge, as HQ is known, is in my opinion a hideous 1970s sectional concrete construction. It spoils some beautiful woodland seven miles north of Nottingham and looks as though it could have been thrown together by some idiot TV personality on *Blue Peter*, or a design student working through a debilitating migraine. It has recently been painted a deep blue on the outside in a hopeless attempt at smartening it up.

As soon as I joined I was told that Sherwood Lodge was where all the chief officers and their hand-picked staff hid from police work and as such proper police officers below the rank of sergeant were not permitted to work there. I quickly learned that it was commonly known by front line officers as 'Fraggle Rock' from *The Muppets*, and also by some as 'The Dream Factory'. This was due to the fact that some police officers apparently spent their entire careers there, climbing the ranks and then disappearing, fulfilling their own personal dreams, avoiding shifts and the thoroughly distasteful nature of proper police work. So I was told. At first I didn't understand this level of antipathy towards others, mainly due to the natural deference in which I held those of a higher status than myself. I was still very naïve. So when you read the words Fraggle Rock you'll know what I'm referring to. Senior officers above the rank of sergeant were also known as 'gaffers', and so I will refer to them as such from now on.

Apart from the mounted section as was, with their stables in the woods, there was also a dog section, with their kennels. Uniform stores and the Scenes of Crime departments were also based there, as was the twenty-four-hour Force Control Room. In those days each of the forty-three forces in England and Wales were completely autonomous with all their own equipment and facilities. They also therefore had their own reputations, which were jealously guarded.

I had an informal twenty-minute interview with the assistant chief constable, then almost immediately afterwards I was instructed to visit the stores department for a uniform. It seemed I had indeed been given the job.

I was issued my unique collar number, which would

stay with me for the next thirty years and by which I would be identified, very often without an accompanying name. I would be known as PC 512, a mere number, like Patrick McGoohan's character in the '60s television series *The Prisoner*, known as Number Six, or Charlton Heston's galley slave, number forty-one, in the movie *Ben-Hur*. I wasn't sure of the reasons for having this unique number; I don't think we were told. It could be in case I shared a common surname with another officer, which sometimes happens. It could also be in case of impropriety on my part, presumably if I swore at a member of the public – or worse – this number would be visible to all. It was part of being absorbed into the whole, like falling victim to the Borg in *Star Trek*. There is no human being attached, you are a number, and a resource. Resistance is futile, though quite how futile I wasn't to know at the time. I should have realised that as with life among the Borg, independent thought of any kind is frowned upon, and expressions of it can cause serious problems. The same applies to common sense too, but I didn't know that either.

I was very slim in those days, almost six feet tall and my ribs were visible like those of a prize greyhound or a camp survivor. The brand new black uniform fitted very well. I looked and felt extremely smart, like an SS tank commander. There is definitely something psychologically affecting about putting on a smart, well-fitting uniform. The Nazis clearly realised this when they hired the German fashion designer Hugo Boss to create their uniforms. The silver buttons on the front of my crisp tunic sparkled in the bright lights of the fitting-room, and I could hardly believe what was happening. The smell of the new wool fabric filled the air and added to the pleasant atmosphere of the stores department. Several mature ladies were sitting in open offices quietly sewing uniforms with BBC Radio Two audible in the background. All was calm and clean, and it reminded me of a kibbutz clinic.

I signed a huge sheet of lined card several times with my name and collar number to say that I'd received my great coat, two tunics, two pairs of heavy woollen uniform trousers (no concessions to hot weather in those days), five pale blue shirts, two clip-on black ties, a pair of black leather gloves, and a pair of thin white gloves for formal parades, funerals and other special occasions. I was handed a brand new wooden truncheon with leather strap, shiny with wood grain like a chestnut, and a pair of chain-link chrome-plated steel handcuffs. I was given the keys to the handcuffs along with a universal 'police key' which opened the doors to all police stations in the county. Finally I was given a helmet, with 'Nottinghamshire Constabulary' written in a circle inside the crest. I was told to buy my own boots from an army stores.

My first full day in uniform soon followed, when I spent two weeks at the lovely Force Training School, Epperstone Manor, on an 'Initial Course'. There were eleven of us, of which three were female, known in those days as WPCs. We each signed up for some small monthly pay deductions such as 'Retirement Fund', 'Death grant fund', 'St George's Fund', and 'Convalescent Home', though I wasn't sure what these were for at the time. To my pleasant surprise we were informed that our bank accounts would be credited with £163 advance pay for the latter half of the current month. I was delighted with this, as to me it was a small fortune. Three days later we swore an Oath of Office at the old Shire Hall Magistrates Court in

Nottingham, which is now a museum called 'The Galleries of Justice':

'Do you solemnly and sincerely declare and affirm that you will well and truly serve Our Sovereign Lady The Queen in the Office of Constable, without fear or affection, malice or ill-will, and that you will to the best of your power cause the Peace to be kept and preserved, and prevent all offences against the persons and properties of Her Majesty's Subjects: and that while you continue to hold said office, you will to the best of your skill and knowledge discharge all the duties thereof faithfully according to Law.'

I found it interesting that this oath was completely apolitical and we were not swearing any allegiance to the government of the day, or even to parliament. Her Majesty the Queen was therefore our ultimate boss. The Crown symbol was everywhere on our uniforms, on every button on the tunic, including the sleeves and the pockets, and of course the helmet. Take a few moments to look at a modern British cop and you will notice the difference. They all look like members of the SAS, without a crown in sight.

The pub in Epperstone was called The Cross Keys, and we grew to know it very well. I was with a great bunch of people, and it soon became clear who was destined to achieve higher rank. Both Tony and Joanne always did very well in exams and written work, which they seemed to finish very quickly, while I struggled, completely unused to anything of this sort since schooldays six years before. Picking fruit in Israel and lying on Bondi beach for months did little to prepare me for the pressured training environment. I remember Tony was questioned as to why one of his exam results had slipped back to a disappointing 98%. "Where were the other 2%?" he was asked.

At the end of the first two weeks' residential course, we

were given our instructions for the main block of training at the Regional Police Training Centre, starting the following Monday morning. At that time, for Nottinghamshire officers, it meant a two-hour drive up the A1 motorway to North Yorkshire, to a windswept military base called RAF Dishforth.

TRAINING SCHOOL

RAF DISHFORTH

I shared a car with two Daves from my Initial Course. Tall Dave had a bushy moustache and smoked *Embassy Number 1s*, and small Dave, who was ex-Royal Navy, also had an enormous moustache with the addition of long sideburns. He was wiry and light on his feet like Burt Kwok, Peter Seller's manservant in the *Pink Panther* films. He was therefore nicknamed 'Dave Kato-sideburns', despite not being in any way of Oriental heritage. I didn't as yet own a car, so I was happy to travel in tall Dave's bright red 1981 Ford Cortina Mark V with beige vinyl roof.

I also had a thick black moustache at the time, so the three of us probably looked like extras from a gay porn movie or the campest half of a Village People tribute act, as we trundled northwards in our bright red Cortina. This first unfamiliar journey was incredibly tedious, and we all dreaded the prospect of repeating the same trip every week for the next *thirteen weeks.*

We eventually found RAF Dishforth in the bleak emptiness of North Yorkshire, and Dave parked the car close to the main gate. We reported to the guardroom where we found a huge handlebar moustache with a man attached to it sitting at a table facing the door. He had great wads of printed lists in front of him and a fountain pen in his right hand. He was flanked on either side by men in police sergeant's uniforms with stern faces like night club bouncers. A thick filter-less cigarette, probably a *Capstan Full Strength*, was perched on the rim of a near-full ashtray, burning away with a length of ash an inch long about to fall.

We each volunteered our names and the huge moustachioed man behind the desk grunted unintelligibly, drew some squiggles on the papers in front of him then handed us a sheet each. These were our instructions with details of class numbers and accommodation blocks. It seemed we were being split up. I took my copy of the first week's timetable and walked out the door with the Daves. I crossed a section of neatly cropped grass near the guardroom and suddenly I heard a loud screaming female voice from somewhere behind me:

"Oy, you! Get off the grass!" I looked around to see a female police sergeant in a blue uniform, glaring at me and pointing in my direction.

"Blimey, alright, sarge…" I replied, chuntering to myself, making an effort to clear the grass onto the car park.

"Alright, *SERGEANT*!" she shouted in response, as loud as her first command. *What a horrible woman!* I thought to myself. I hoped I'd never see that particular person again, even if she did have an enormous chest.

I found my billet, a building called Hurricane Block, located on Chantmarle Avenue. It still had faded camouflage on the outside walls like every other wartime RAF base. My iron-framed bed was in an open dormitory with a dozen others and on one side was a small chest of drawers, on the other a wardrobe. The furniture was functional if a little tired and was probably still RAF property. Having spent several week-long summer camps at various RAF bases in the air cadets, everything seemed vaguely familiar. If I'd fallen asleep and woken up suddenly I could have been forgiven for thinking I'd joined the air force, but the Spartan conditions were no real problem, having lived as a stateless vagrant for so long.

The first afternoon was not particularly taxing. We were herded like sheep into a large room while frequently barked at by various angry sergeants. The man with the handlebar moustache appeared, now looking as though he'd stepped off the set of the film *Carry on up the Khyber*. He wore a sergeant's uniform, must have been at least fifty, and was wielding an army sergeant major's yard stick with polished chrome at both ends. He told us we couldn't walk on any of the grassed areas and that we were to march everywhere when in uniform, rather than "walking about looking like Saturday night Jessies out on the piss..."

He told us we had to salute everyone above the rank of sergeant, and we were not permitted to shout or otherwise bring ourselves into disrepute in the eyes of the RAF personnel with whom we shared the camp. It was their home, and we were their guests. Someone should have reminded the RAF of these rules; only a few days later as our small group marched quietly past the canteen block a member of the RAF leaned out from a window and shouted at someone in the near distance: *"You fucking cock-sucker!"* The window slammed shut and we all burst out laughing.

The elderly sergeant told us that we were to stand up immediately when anyone above our lowly rank of constable entered the room, wherever we were. Male officers were strictly forbidden from entering the female dorms, and any sexual fraternisation between males and females would result in serious trouble. It was assumed the female candidates would not wish to enter the male dorms, so a warning against this was never given. Neither was a warning about males becoming amorous with other males or any other same sex encounter. I think it was just assumed this wouldn't happen. He then went on to inform us that just like him we would all most likely acquire stomach ulcers and gout later in our service, an inevitable result of being on your feet all day and breathing in fumes at busy road junctions while directing traffic. He said all this in-between long pulls on a *Capstan Full Strength*, which he cupped inside one hand, the smoke curling around his sleeve as it rose up his arm. His health problems were apparently not connected to drinking and smoking.

We then had a welcome briefing by the camp commander; a man who looked and sounded very similar to the empty-headed Captain Ashwood in the comedy series *It Ain't Half Hot, Mum*. He wasn't particularly camp, and he didn't look like a commander of any sort. He was a superintendent, apparently, and I never saw him again.

In the evenings, a routine developed which became an integral part of life at Dishforth. We all gathered around in groups 'bulling' our boots and discussing the day. Spit and polish was whirled around endlessly with clean yellow dusters in fine circles on the toe-caps of our boots which eventually caused the surface of the leather to shine like glass. The thick woollen uniform trousers were pressed repeatedly, with some students rubbing soap down the inside crease to gain a sharper line. The air in the dorm became heavy with a nightly mix of *Kiwi* polish, cigarette smoke and ironing. I really did feel as though I was back at an air cadet summer camp.

There wasn't a lot of individual privacy, and it soon became clear how many lads supplemented their diet with what they could harvest from their nose, chewing loudly as they did so, licking their lips for more, and disposing of unwanted excess on the bedclothes or smearing it onto nearby furniture. Quite a few snored like walruses from the minute they were asleep until they were awake the next morning.

Nudity was something I had to get used to, and I am always surprised by some men's obvious pride when displaying their genitalia, wandering about the dorm completely naked or naked from the waist *down,* rather than the waist up, their parts flopping about all over the place. Was this *never* done deliberately I wonder?

Just before lights out, the chap in the opposite bunk placed his sweaty socks over the iron radiator next to his bed. The musty, cheesy aroma of this man's feet then drifted around the room like a pernicious cloud. According to him they would then be fresh again for the morning. I noticed he did this every night with what appeared to be the *same* pair of socks, for the entire fourteen weeks.

A thin, pale-skinned lad from Yorkshire in the bed diagonally opposite seemed to have trouble gathering his thoughts every morning. He'd sit on his bed, both feet flat to the floor with his head in his hands completely immobile until the very last minute when he would quickly get dressed without any kind of wash, then run down the stairs with the rest of us.

Day and night I heard some astonishing farting and belching, some of which seemed to be generated on command with tonal qualities and pitch control. Bearing in mind it was mid-winter, so there wasn't a single window open. "Breathe it in, quick! Get rid of it!" was the usual cry. It's not entirely true that 'all coppers are wankers', but in the middle of the night when they think everyone else is asleep some clearly are. Such was life in a men's dormitory.

A good deal of mutual piss-taking and towel-slapping took place, but there was generally a good atmosphere and I don't remember any of us falling out or even arguing about anything. We became a cohesive unit, living and working together and borrowing one another's kit, right down to blobs of toothpaste and squirts of shaving foam. I slowly began to feel part of something that was much bigger than me, and I think we all felt the same.

There was a very nice bar on the camp, known as The Packhorse Club, and it was clearly once a full-time air force NAAFI pub. It was large, welcoming and very well stocked. There were strict opening times of between 8pm and 10.30pm daily. We all made great use of it that first Monday night and indeed most subsequent nights, perhaps far too much.

Reveille was at 6.30am every morning, and you couldn't miss it. Numerous loud bells were set off throughout the block like a fire alarm, and a sergeant came stomping into the dormitory prodding each bed with a long stick, shouting the same endearing cry:

"Hands off cocks, hands on socks! Get up gentlemen, outside in fifteen minutes!"

It seemed like the middle of the night. A dark North Yorkshire airfield shrouded in freezing fog is as far removed from Bondi beach as is possible to be. Somewhere under the many layers of uniform there were faded tan lines around my bottom from months of Australian sun. We stood in lines with vacuously empty stomachs, painfully hung over and freezing cold. I think my teeth actually chattered a little.

We were introduced to the pleasures of drill, marching pointlessly up and down in unison like robots. Thankfully

I'd done a lot in the air cadets and a little at Epperstone, so I knew what to expect, but most of the others hadn't a clue. Some tried marching with their left hand forward in time with the left leg, and others just couldn't keep a rhythm, despite some alarming hopping movements. Thick fog covered everything like dry ice at a Pink Floyd concert, and it seemed for a few moments I was in the army preparing for Arctic manoeuvres. I pulled at the ends of my black leather gloves to give my fingers some relief, and I could feel the bones in my face contract as though deep-sea diving. It was quite literally freezing cold.

After what seemed hours, but was in fact only about thirty minutes, we were marched along Bruche Drive in small groups to the canteen block known as Rowan House. Breakfast was served promptly between 7.30am and 7.45am. If you ever missed it – which was unlikely – then you would remain hungry all day. The dining hall was humid and pungent with the wonderful smell of hot fat and buttered toast. There were masses of fried food in shallow stainless steel containers. The original steel-framed, single-glazed windows streamed with condensation, and the room was packed with RAF personnel at the far end, loud and raucous, paying us no attention at all. We jostled one another with our plastic trays, eagerly queuing up for food.

We sat in the warmth slowly defrosting, immediately shovelling down huge quantities of fried bread, eggs, bacon, sausages, beans, tomatoes and black pudding. I had difficulty flexing my fingers enough to grip the cutlery, and as I looked around I could see the faces of my colleagues beginning to glow. We ate in a furious manner, as though we'd just been rescued from the Stalingrad *kessel*. We drank lots of sweet tea, and those who had them took out their cigarettes. The

LESSONS IN LAW

Classes started at 9am, and we had to be seated by 8.50am. I was in classroom V in Provost Block. I had two dedicated tutors, both sergeants. One was called Andy, and was from my own force. The other was female and called Jane, from West Yorkshire. As Jane appeared I realised she was the same gobby female sergeant with the big tits who had shouted at me on arrival. I doubt she remembered me. She didn't seem to, anyway.

Our first lesson was given by her, and was on police regulations and restrictions on the private life of a constable. I had no idea. I don't remember anyone warning me about these restrictions. From now on I couldn't take any active part in politics, which meant I couldn't even join a political party, even a mainstream party. I had to ask permission from the police to buy a house, to rent one or even to move house, and they had to approve the location when I did. Permission was needed to marry, or even co-habit, and the name of any prospective spouse was to be supplied for checking and approval. I was not permitted to take on any financial indebtedness other than a lawful debt from a reputable lender, or take part in anything which could be perceived to put the impartiality of my office at risk. All lawful debts were to be repaid on time or disciplinary action could follow. I was forbidden from borrowing money from a colleague, and on or off duty I should not behave in any manner which had potential to bring the service into disrepute.

That's *potential*, including *actual.* There's clearly *potential* in anything we do, and I didn't realise the seriousness of this at first. On reflection, it seems remarkable that this was the first thing we were taught.

We were told Leon Britten was the Home Secretary of the day, and therefore our political master in charge of all policing issues. We noted all the pertinent facts in longhand using fountain pens in HMSO A4 notebooks, supplied free of charge. We were told the officer on the beat is the most important person in the police force, and that all the law and procedure we were being taught was expected to be thoroughly understood. The definitions of important offences were learnt verbatim such as theft, burglary, deception, and so on. We were instructed how to take an emergency phone call from a member of the public, and how to maintain a pocket notebook. The use of typing fluid was strictly forbidden when keeping a pocket book, as was removing a page or leaving gaps. Each page of the police pocket book was sequentially numbered so it occurred to me that if one was ripped out it would be blatantly obvious. At the time, the comedy stage show *The Secret Policeman's Ball* was jokingly sponsored by Tippex.

I found the lessons quite interesting. Except for the ones which followed a heavy lunch when I struggled to stay awake. I learnt how to yawn with my mouth completely shut, venting the subsequent air pressure through my nostrils in a well-practiced technique. It meant some rather strange facial distortions where I probably looked like a closed-mouth version of Donald Sutherland's character at the end of the movie *Invasion of the Body Snatchers*. I was once caught and shouted at: "If you don't open your mouth your bloody head will explode!"

We had very little interview training, which I found surprising. We were told some very basic psychology associated with it, such as if the suspect fidgets a lot and was sweating then they were clearly telling lies. The admission was everything, and you must obtain 'the cough' at all costs, as nothing else mattered. Fingerprints were the only other form of evidence, but these seemed secondary to the all-important cough. We learnt a code of conduct known as 'Judge's Rules' which seemed vague and nebulous in nature, but the main thing I took from this was the fact that the judge was at the top of the judicial system, and was therefore all-powerful.

The importance of the caution was discussed, to be issued as soon as the person was suspected of committing an offence. The differences between Common, Statute and Case Laws were also revealed. We had to make sure we knew the phonetic Morse code, which I did anyway from my air cadet days. We learnt of the different uniform roles within the police service, such as the beat officer, the area constable, and the car beat constable who drove around in a panda car. The 'panda' car was so called because the doors were black and the rest of the vehicle was white or pale blue. This is not to be confused with the 'jam sandwich', which was the larger traffic car. This had a red or orange stripe around the middle, and was white everywhere else.

Then there was the role of the CID, the Criminal Investigation Department, joining which was considered to be a positive move, almost like a promotion, even if you remained at the same rank. I was to realise later that some constables really did think they had been promoted when they went onto the CID and ditched their uniforms for good. Quite often they would expect you to open the door for them in the station; some of them had climbed so very far up their own backsides they lost sight of daylight and behaved as though they were being filmed for an episode of *The Sweeney*, wandering about full of their own self-importance.

We were told of the collator's role in the station, a job usually undertaken by a uniformed officer with a considerable amount of service who invariably knew all the local villains and where they lived, because he'd most likely dealt with them personally in his long career. The collator at each station maintained a comprehensive hand-written card index system of addresses, and this was used to assist in any crime enquiries. 'Liaison with Collator' was one of the ticky-box questions on the back of every crime report. I imagined that perhaps when I was very old and reaching fifty years of age there'd be a job for me as a collator, with no shift work and permanently in the station warm and dry.

I was very impressed with the PNC, the Police National Computer, introduced ten years before, in 1974. Though I'd not seen it yet, it sounded like an incredible machine, with all the country's vehicles recorded, thousands of criminal names, and all at the touch of a button. We had lengthy lectures on how to take a good witness statement, including validity of evidence, hearsay, points to prove, opinions, and the value of setting the scene and obtaining good descriptions. A statement was just like a story which you had to write quickly and accurately, often in difficult circumstances. I enjoyed this because it was like being taught observation skills and professional writing. I never tired of writing statements, for obvious reasons, and would always volunteer when necessary. 'Fred Smith hit me,' would be the main evidence in an assault statement against Mr Smith, but it is clearly insufficient. Where was the aggrieved when it happened? Was he at home, in a pub, in the street? Had he been drinking? What time was it? Who was he with? What was he doing? Did he know Fred Smith, and if so how? What did Smith use as a weapon? Where did he hit you? Did it hurt? Did you provoke him? Did you hit back?

The treatment of prisoners and their rights were discussed, though not in great length. To be brutally frank I don't think they had many rights at the time. We were told that if necessary a person could be restrained using handcuffs, and if convenient they could be escorted on foot to the nearest police station. An arrested person was a 'prisoner', not a 'detainee' and very definitely not a 'customer' as they are sometimes referred to today. There were varying degrees of contempt for anyone who had chosen to break the law and feelings of sympathy were not encouraged, unless it was fake sympathy in order to obtain the cough.

The days rolled into weeks, punctuated by the drive home every Friday evening and the return on Sunday nights. On each Monday morning there was a written multiple choice exam of the previous weeks' input. I've never been good at exams, always a popular excuse used by thick people like me who find them difficult. I should have seated myself closer to the front of the examination hall. A colleague told me years later that he could see the answer papers on the examiner's desk so he cheated in every single exam.

At the end of the fourth week I spent the entire weekend at home in bed with a chest infection. It was quite serious and on the Saturday evening my parents were forced to call the emergency doctor as I had real trouble breathing. I was dosed up on antibiotics and painkillers and just managed to get back to Dishforth in time on Monday morning. Unfortunately it was the first of the four-weekly ‘stage exams’. It came as no surprise that I failed it, as I’d spent most of the weekend unconscious rather than revising. I took it again later in the day with all the other ‘dippers’ and passed. It was obvious I wasn’t well. There was a real danger I’d be re-coursed, or worse, so I tried my best to carry on, despite feeling terrible. Luckily I was excused PT and swimming during that fifth week, and by the following weekend I was fully recovered.

I still didn’t feel like a police officer. We had no idea what it was like; I don’t suppose any of us did, except those who had already been police cadets. We hadn’t as yet done anything, or more accurately, *done anyone* for anything. Like actors in an empty theatre, we were always in dress rehearsal.

Eventually it was announced that we would undertake some role-playing. They were officially called practical tests, and I was struck by just how much it was like acting. An instructor in plain clothes drove a very old Austin 1100 similar to that driven by John Cleese in *Fawlty Towers* around the narrow camp roads, pretending to be a member of the public. Huddled together in our little groups we each took it in turn to stand in the road and use the number one stop signal, right arm raised with flat palm facing the driver. We then had to find offences connected to the driver’s use of the vehicle. These were known as ‘Construction and Use’ offences. There’d be a bald tyre somewhere, the tax disc might be missing, there’d be a broken light, or the driver would very coyly admit to not having a driving licence. I thought this was excellent, the way offenders would just admit things straight away.

On one occasion we were quite shocked when the driver stated he couldn’t get out of the vehicle because he was too drunk to move. It was only right that people should be honest with police officers, as who would dare tell outright fibs to an officer of the law? People clearly had an innate sense of wanting to help the police and coughed everything immediately.

We noted down the important facts in our pocket books and after each minor drama we returned to the classroom and composed witness statements from an evidential point of view, without irrelevant opinion or hearsay. Unless it was an opinion of a person's intoxication; this is one of the few professional opinions an ordinary police officer can give that is valid in court.

Gradually as the weeks passed these practical scenarios became longer, more elaborate, and with the law becoming increasingly technical. I found the traffic side of the job crushingly boring. Kerb-side and gross weights, the different types of HGV and PSV licences and so on, just didn't stay in my head. I became more interested in crime because it seemed more straightforward and easier to remember.

On 16th April 1984 we were given the following statistics:

Reported crime in 1984 in England & Wales is broken down as follows:

Theft & handling stolen goods: 54.1%
Burglary: 24.4%
Criminal damage: 13.0%
Fraud & forgery: 3.6%
Violence against person: 3.4%
Robbery: 0.7%
Sexual offences: 0.7%
Others: 1.0%

The figures were meaningless other than to demonstrate the type of offences we were likely to come across. Theft and burglary would be the most common, and anything such as robbery, sexual offences and fraud would be dealt with by those clever people in the CID. We were told that most criminals were from a working class background, and that Nottinghamshire shared some of the highest crime rates in the country, at 7,500 per 100,000 of population, in common with Merseyside, London, Manchester and Northumbria. It seemed that most posh people never encountered the police, and so by implication never broke the law.

Offences of assault were covered, including sexual offences. A person could never consent to assault, even in the bedroom and in private. 'Unnatural' sexual offences were discussed which mainly consisted of buggery with another person or with an animal, both of which seemed to be categorised together and were therefore seen as equally bad. Sodomy was discussed, and was defined as: 'Sexual intercourse per anus between males or male and female'. It was a serious crime, an arrestable offence, i.e., it carried a prison sentence of five years, and was illegal even with a spouse. Consent, apparently, was no defence.

There were some lawful homosexual acts, but they must take place in private, with the consent of both parties, and a maximum of two persons taking part, both being male and over twenty-one years of age. There was an excellent mnemonic to remember this: Private, Over 21, Only 2, and Full consent: POOF.

It has never been a crime for two females to have sex with each other. Most British sexual offences legislation originated in Victorian times, when it was assumed such things didn't happen. It was deemed to be a criminal offence to have sex with any close member of your own family, except your grandmother, should you fancy it.

A wife was chattel and belonged to her husband. He could therefore never be guilty of the offence of rape against her. How times have changed.

SWIMMING AND FIGHTING

We did a lot of swimming, usually at Thirsk baths when sessions were closed to the public. This was always straight after a huge breakfast, or a heavy lunch with jam sponge pudding for desert. I enjoyed the swimming, mainly because I was good at it, having previously spent a lot of time splashing about on some of the greatest beaches in the world. We had to retrieve a black plastic brick from the deep end of the pool while wearing pyjamas, something I found very easy, but was a difficult task for some. We had races against the clock and formed swimming teams. We were also taught life-saving, which consisted of hauling a colleague in his or her pyjamas across the pool merely by gripping the underside of their chin with the fingers of one hand.

The return journey to Dishforth was usually very quiet, with the windows of the bus running with condensation from fifty wet heads and our exhausted breathing. Absorbing information after this was particularly challenging. These were usually the most common occasions I'd practice my closed-mouth *Body Snatchers* yawning technique.

We acquired some useful first aid knowledge, and we also took part in self-defence classes. I found this choreographed wrestling quite difficult to remember. We had to learn things such as 'wrist twist', 'wrist turn', 'side arm lock', 'arm entanglement', 'cross-block front pull-down', 'cross-block rear pull-down', and 'shirt grab release'. I couldn't even remember the names let alone the moves. If they'd asked me to perform a cross-block wrist twist bum's rush I'd give it a go. Whatever it was it usually ended up with everyone rolling around on the floor. The PT instructors were ruthless and unsympathetic. While struggling with one of these movements and taking extra time to finish, I was shouted at from across the gym on more than one occasion:

"There's a factory not far from here where they make fireworks. You need to go there and get yourself a rocket so you can stuff it up your bloody arse!"

There were some quite frightening scenarios where we were expected to fight a colleague one-to-one, then two-to-one, and ultimately try to defend ourselves with bare hands against four simultaneous attackers from all angles. The only concession to health and safety seemed to be a rubber mat on the floor barely an inch thick. There was usually a catalogue of minor injuries and sprains following each session.

If you were caught with your arms folded even for a second you were ordered to "Give me ten!" by one of the PT instructors, meaning you then had to get down onto the floor and perform ten press-ups. If you let out a 'tut' or showed any dissent whatsoever it then became "Give me twenty!" Having done this once I rose to my feet and found my arms ached so much I instinctively folded them again, thereby inviting a further twenty press-ups as punishment. I tutted out loud at my own stupidity and I was then given another twenty. By the time I'd finished I felt utterly exhausted and didn't know what to do with my arms.

We were sometimes ordered to crawl across the full length of the hardwood gym floor using our elbows to haul ourselves along, which was as excruciating as it was pointless. There was a wall at one side of the gym about seven feet high to a viewing gallery, and quite at random we were frequently ordered to run straight at it and climb over. It wasn't easy, but we all managed it, eventually. Anyone who struggled even briefly was mercilessly derided by the instructors and named 'Chris Bonnington', which was the name of a famous British mountain climber at the time.

In the cross-country runs I usually did well, and on one occasion I finished in second place in the whole course. It seemed my lungs were recovering from the effects of five years' smoking. We sometimes played softball on a playing field near Dishforth's runway. On rare days of fine weather, Jet Provost aircraft would repeatedly perform 'circuits and bumps', and my mind would wander to the pilots inside the aircraft: numerous safety checks, shouts of "More power!" and "Pull back gently on the stick!" and so on, then back to the officers' mess for tea and biccies.

Our final practical test involved one of the largest male sergeants pretending to be drunk, wandering around the streets of Dishforth in jeans and a football shirt, complete with a glass bottle in one hand, singing away loudly, occasionally shouting obscenities. I was chosen to sort this person out. I tried verbal reasoning and was promptly told to "Fuck off" several times. I grabbed one of his arms and immediately found that he was as immovable as a tree. He was deliberately blocking my attempts at putting a wrist lock or arm entanglement on him, or even a bum's rush. His limbs were rigid and I wondered whether a man as drunk as this would have all his faculties about him as he did. I swung from his arm like a rag doll, and made no progress in suppressing him at all. It didn't occur to me to remove the wooden stick from inside my right trouser leg and hit him with it, or to trip him and push him to the floor. He was a colleague after all, and he was only acting. Maybe if he'd hit me and caused me to feel some pain then I could have handled it better. It was just not in my nature to be violent, even less to be able to turn it on at will. Until that moment I could count on one hand just how many times in my life I'd seriously lost my temper.

After about five minutes a truce was called and it was declared a draw. I felt embarrassed that I'd not subdued the man and handcuffed him. But he didn't get away, no-one was hurt, and so it was a satisfactory conclusion of sorts. From that moment on I wondered what would happen when I inevitably faced the same scenario in the real world.

After the tenth week it seemed I might make it to the end of the course after all, so I felt able to risk a bank loan. I bought my first car. I wanted a brand new car, but I didn't want to pay too much for it, so I bought a Citroen 2CV. It was £3,400, and was called a *Beachcomber.* It was white with two wavy blue lines running over the top from front to back, like D-Day invasion stripes. It looked like a massive blob of toothpaste, and it appeared very gay indeed, in both senses of the word. I drove to Dishforth for the last three weeks in my little car, which had a top speed of 72mph, downhill, with a favourable wind. It was fun to drive, and it was different. I didn't want an old Ford Cortina, and I wasn't bothered about speed. Tall Dave sat in it with a bemused expression on his face, and trying to be polite said: "Well, at least it *smells* like a new car."

The night before graduation we had an end of course fancy dress party in The Packhorse Club. I went as *The Riddler* from the Batman television series. I'd often commented to my classmates that I found many of the exam questions unnecessarily complex, more like riddles, hence the attire. That night the discipline was relaxed, and we were allowed to address the sergeants by their first names. We all stood together on the dance floor with linked arms singing 'You'll Never Walk Alone', encouraged by the instructors. There was a palpable sense of camaraderie between us.

As a result of all the choreographed fighting in the gym I was surprised to find out that we'd qualified as orange belts in Jujitsu. I thought it had all just been a lot of sweaty wrestling sessions and had no idea it was for a formal qualification. We'd also gained recognised qualifications in First Aid and Life Saving, from the hours we spent partially drowning one another in Thirsk baths.

On Friday the 8th June my parents witnessed me marching smartly across the parade square at RAF Dishforth with the rest of the sixty-six males and sixteen females of Course 2/84. Luckily the day was fine and dry, with cotton wool clumps of fair-weather cumulus floating by on a warm summer breeze. It was a proud moment. I had transformed myself from an unemployed travelling vagrant into a police officer. We all felt very professional, disciplined and extremely proud to be wearing the uniform. But I still didn't feel like a copper, and I didn't really know what it was like to be one either.

The following Monday I started another two weeks at Epperstone Manor, on a residential Local Procedure Course, in the company of the ten candidates I'd started with. We familiarised ourselves with the forms used by Nottinghamshire Constabulary and their methods of policing: crime reports, prosecution papers, road accident forms, property handling forms and so on. Each of the forty-three forces in England and Wales had their own unique methods at that time as there was little or no national or even regional standardisation. A crime file consisted of a pink front, synopsis, witness statement(s), contemporaneous interview notes, exhibits and a list of the offender's convictions in full for the court to examine. It was years before the national standardised MG series.

Near the car park of the old manor there was a small open-air swimming pool. It was clean and ready for use but it was unheated. We celebrated the end of the course by jumping in. This was a tradition, apparently. I was very glad it was summer!

We were given just over a week off and our start date in the real world was Monday 2nd July. I'd grown up in Sheffield, and it was an accident of geography that caused me to join the police in Nottinghamshire. I imagined I'd be given a pedal cycle and told to ride around the small market town of Retford and the quiet leafy lanes of the surrounding villages where my parents lived. But the postings list revealed I was being sent to inner-city Nottingham, a place called Hyson Green. I didn't know the area, and the name made it sound lovely. I had absolutely no idea what was coming.

POSTING

GREGORY BOULEVARD

I needed somewhere to live close to my workplace. Hyson Green was a forty-five minute drive from my parents' house in north Nottinghamshire. I drove into Nottingham and bought an *A to Z* map from a newsagent. I was shocked when I saw the area for the first time. It didn't look anything like the quiet villages around Retford. Adjacent to Hyson Green was a suburb called Forest Fields, which also sounded lovely, so I drove there to take a look. I found dark rows of Victorian red-brick terraced houses adjacent to an open space of green called The Forest. This was a large playing field rising up on one side, some of which was covered in mature deciduous trees. Part of the flat area was the site of the annual Goose Fair. I bought a local paper, the *Nottingham Evening Post* and scanned the property section.

The first flat I visited was the one I moved into. It was a self-contained rooftop bedsit above a large private house in the Mapperley Park area of Nottingham. It was close to Hyson Green but still a discreet distance away. A huge churchy door in a high wall off the main road led up a winding path through a dense garden to the house. On the left was the door to my flat, up a steep staircase that was entirely separate from the rest of the house. The family were clearly quite wealthy and seemed pleased a young policeman was interested in their flat. We liked one another immediately and after fifteen minutes of discussion I was offered an initial six month lease. All I needed then was permission from my employers.

My official posting was given as 'Radford Road'. I had no idea at the time why I'd been sent to an inner-city station, when many of my training school colleagues had been sent to rural or semi-rural locations. Perhaps it was my dark-skinned recruitment photograph and the bizarre way the police even today put ethnic minority officers in similar areas. I decided to find the police station and introduce myself in advance of the actual day I was due to start.

I found Radford Road but as I drove along the full length of it, probably just over a mile, I couldn't find anything that looked like a police station. There was a large square building in the final stages of construction on a corner looking very much like a fortress, but there wasn't a blue lamp outside or any other indication as to what it was. I pulled in to a petrol station near some gasworks and asked the large sweaty man behind the counter, who replied:

"You mean the cop shop on Gregory Boulevard. The new one's not open yet. Go to the end and turn left at the lights. Good luck, you'll fuckin' need it!"

I drove slowly along Gregory Boulevard and found a small sectional concrete building near a tall block of flats. I saw the word 'Police' in small letters on the wall. Part of the sign was missing and the remainder was covered in thick layers of accumulated dirt. There was nowhere to park at the front so I drove around the back. Everything at ground level was covered in graffiti.

I found parking for less than a dozen cars but I managed to squeeze my narrow 2CV into an area that was probably not a designated space. The shabby two-storey police station was tightly sandwiched between other similar buildings, and rubbish was strewn about everywhere. The smell of my new car was replaced by an unpleasant mix of traffic fumes, fried food, cigarettes and decay. I opened the back door of the building using my brand new police key and stepped inside.

All was quiet, and as far as I could work out, there were only two people on the ground floor; a woman in civilian clothes seated at a desk near the public counter and a uniformed sergeant probably in his late thirties in a small office. Both were busy with typewriters and the sergeant's one-fingered tapping came to a stop when I stuck my head around the corner. I introduced myself to them both and we shook hands. Joan smiled and seemed really nice and the sergeant then suggested we go up to the canteen and make tea.

I followed him up the creaking wooden stairs; the linoleum was filthy and worn out, in common with the rest of the building. I was led into a small kitchenette area which had only two round tables and half a dozen chairs. At the sink, the sergeant turned on the tap.

"We're moving out soon. Two weeks actually. Down the road to the new building. Have you seen it? The CID are already there."

"Yes, I have, I think so," I said, remembering the square fortress I'd seen near the petrol station. "Is it the new building on the corner?" I asked as he switched on the kettle.

"Yeah, that's it. It'll be great to get away from this shithole. The local fuckin' snaffs never leave us alone here. Every time you leave your car it gets damaged. We had bricks and bottles chucked over the other day. They really fuckin' hate us. Still, you'll probably be based up at Broxtowe, not round here."

I hadn't a clue what he was saying. Something about cars getting damaged. His candour shocked me. I glanced out the window at my 2CV. The sergeant filled two mugs just as his blue *Burndept* radio crackled loudly with some urgent shouting.

"Sorry, I've got to go, there's just been a till snatch up the road. Help yourself to tea, there's milk in the fridge, there…" and he ran out of the room thudding down the stairs as though taking four at a time. Looking out the back window I saw him in the driver's seat of a panda car, revving the engine and shouting into his radio. The car was a pale blue Vauxhall Chevette with white doors and a rectangular box on the roof with POLICE written on it. A dim blue lamp on top started rotating slowly as he drove away with loud screeching from the tyres. There was no siren of any sort, not even a two-tone.

I finished making tea and wandered through an empty upstairs towards the front of the building. There didn't seem to be anyone else in the station. I stood at the window overlooking the busy road. This wasn't RAF Dishforth where drivers freely admit they didn't have a driving licence or they were too drunk to get out of their cars. I wasn't sure I was prepared for it. It occurred to me that there was a huge gap between the pretend and the real world. Not only that, what the bloody hell was a 'snaff'?

I moved into my bedsit flat in late June after being granted initial permission. The inspector still had to visit in order to give formal confirmation the address was suitable for a police officer. My first day at Gregory Boulevard police station soon followed. I arrived at 7.30am for an 8am – 4pm day shift. I found the building in an opposite state to my first visit; empty of furniture, but with plenty of staff. There was a tense atmosphere similar to that created by a hastily retreating army. Boxes were being emptied and police officers were tearing up sheets of paper and stuffing them into large bags. It all seemed very chaotic. It might have been easier to have simply set fire to everything, as other retreating armies did.

I was to be assigned a tutor constable who would be my guide for several weeks. Until this period of tutorship was completed I was not expected to venture out on my own. He wasn't at work that day, so I was asked to help move furniture. The inspector spoke to me briefly and introduced himself. He asked about my new address and I arranged for him to visit the next day so that he could inspect it. I helped carry some large grey cabinets into a police van and made more tea.

I was then taken to the new station almost a mile away on Radford Road. It was a superb new building compared to the one we were leaving, which had long-since become unfit for purpose. There were plush new carpets, bright walls, shiny fire doors and new furniture in most of the rooms. It was enormous and seemed entirely self-contained. There was a huge canteen and bar area on the top floor, and in the basement a complex of corridors with male and female cells. Workmen were still wandering around the building, tools in hand, carrying miscellaneous bits of apparel yet to be fixed in somewhere. It was an exciting, busy time. I spent the day carrying things about, and at 4pm my shift was over.

That evening after work I decided I needed to familiarise myself with Nottingham. People would be asking me directions, and at the time I hadn't a clue. I drove my 2CV into Hyson Green, parked outside an off-licence and bought four cans of Australian *Castlemaine XXXX* from a convivial Sikh proprietor. I put the beer on the front seat next to me and drove around the city, trying to remember street names, an open can wedged between my legs.

After a while I fled to the outer suburbs. I found some beautiful rolling countryside on the north eastern edge of the city, hills that reminded me of Sheffield. I put on Roger Waters' new album, *The Pros and Cons of Hitch Hiking,* and drank as I drove around. Memories of hitchhiking around Australia were in my mind, and I felt uneasy about what I was doing in the police. I remembered my brother-in-law's words about leaving anytime, and I thought I might. I needed to give it some time though, but how much? The job was fine so far, but I hadn't done anything yet.

The inspector from Radford Road appeared at my door the next evening. He stayed less than five minutes. He seemed impressed with the flat, despite its modest size. It was in a quiet location, with a private balcony at the top of the house and this was impressive in itself, high amongst the tall trees surrounding the house. This was probably one of the reasons why the rent was so high, at £145 a month. It was a lot considering my salary at the time was less than £400 a month.

I spent a few days at Gregory Boulevard before it was abandoned. The enquiry counter had been almost constantly busy with what I could only describe as socially challenged locals, referred to by colleagues as 'snaffs'. "There's another fucking snaff at the counter…" was the usual comment. Or "I just dealt with this cunt, what a complete fuckin' snaff he was…" and so on. It seemed the hatred reserved for us by the public was entirely mutual. I asked what 'snaff' meant and was told it was Sub Normal and Fucking Useless, a derivative of the Royal Navy expression SNAFU, meaning the same, or similar.

The location of the old police station and the frequency of visitors day and night created a claustrophobic atmosphere as though it was under siege. Joan seemed to be the only female enquiry clerk who worked there, and she was constantly busy. As I shifted furniture around I saw Joan seeing off some particularly unfriendly locals with the help of Jimmy, an amiable red-faced police officer. Jimmy sold me a black leather pocket-book cover for £5 he'd made himself, which amazingly I used right up to my last day in the job. Jimmy and Joan were polite but firm with the customers, if a little sarcastic, but I don't think the visitors ever realised this. If you remain calm and polite, it seems a lot of thick people don't realise you are taking the piss.

The biggest problem the locals had at that time was the loss or theft of their social security cheques, known as giros. They knew that if they could acquire a crime number from the police the social security office would then give them a replacement; hence the near constant queues at the police station. Crime numbers were readily issued in order to get rid of them as quickly as possible, even though fraud was suspected in many cases. Nobody seemed to care about crime rates, nationally or individually. There were no league tables or media comparisons with other forces, so the main concern for cops was simply getting through the shift in order to go home.

Housing, neighbourhood and welfare issues were dealt with at the police station too; lots of problems that were frankly nothing to do with the police. No-one else seemed interested, and the police couldn't escape by shutting their doors at 5pm like other agencies. There were some dire social problems in the area, originating mainly from an enormous 1970s flats complex behind the old station linked together by suspended concrete walkways. It looked incredibly depressing and seemed to be inhabited almost entirely by snaffs and criminals.

When we finally left, there wasn't any closing ceremony at Gregory Boulevard, we simply stopped going there. It was abandoned in a similar manner to when the German 6th Army retreated from Russia, except in our case the locals seemed much more hostile.

The new building on Radford Road was more in the Basford area of Nottingham than Hyson Green, between the Shipstones Brewery and Cussons soap factory, neither of which are functioning today. For years working at Radford Road became synonymous with the not unpleasant aromas of brewing beer and perfumed soap, particularly in summer when the windows were wide open.

I think many of the regular locals thought we'd left the country, because for several weeks after the move very few of them came to see us. Clearly the distance to the new station was just too much. It gave us chance to settle in before the inevitable rush. I never understood the dichotomy here. The police at the time were apparently despised, and yet the very people who had the greatest antipathy towards us were always the most frequent visitors asking for help. I don't think this has changed much.

I made my acquaintance with my tutor constable. He was an extremely tall, bespectacled and moustachioed man in his late thirties known as Roofer Bob. I didn't ask where his nickname originated. I was to be attached to him all the time I was at work, at least for the next few weeks. Sadly we

Bob was almost constantly negative about everything I did, including my attempts at being a police officer. I was criticised harshly and not in any way constructively. I think it is safe to say that I didn't learn anything from him. Later that summer while I was away at training school there was a minor riot in Hyson Green. It wasn't anything on the scale of the Brixton riots but a few windows were broken with bottles and bricks thrown at the police. While I don't wish injury to anyone, least of all a police colleague, Bob took a blow in the face from a brick thrown at him by some anonymous black man. I happen to believe in Karma, so there was some irony in this. Thankfully he was not seriously injured and he made a full recovery. He was then moved away from the city and placed somewhere in the county, though I didn't really care enough to find out. He finished his service in some sleepy English village; presumably well away from people he didn't want to talk to.

I worked my first night shift as a police officer on 9th July 1984. We worked seven consecutive nights in those days, starting at 10pm and finishing at 6am. As the shift 'sprog' it was my duty to arrive half an hour early and make tea for everyone. This was the tradition, and it would be my job until the next sprog arrived on the shift. Night shifts in the police are unlike some industries where you can sleep for a few hours. We were expected to work non-stop all through the night, to be out of the police station all the time, with permission and a good reason required to come back in.

I remember my first night shift trying to fingerprint a prisoner just as dawn lightened the sky at 4.30am. I fiddled with the small tube of fingerprint ink, dabbing it on the copper block then rolling it smooth. I managed to do it right, but I was exhausted and all I wanted to do was go home. I'd worked night shifts before at the kibbutz factory, but they finished at 4am. It seems this time of night is the lowest point for the human body.

Nottinghamshire Police were very busy in the summer of 1984. We were at the centre of a lot of media attention. Leave was heavily restricted, and the first few months of my service at the station were hard work. Soon after starting at Radford Road we began working twelve hour shifts, with only one rest day in every ten. This incurred a huge amount of overtime. The first item of paperwork I became familiar with was the overtime form. The reason of course was that the miners' dispute led by Arthur Scargill and his National Union of Mineworkers had started on 12th March, and it was becoming increasingly bitter. It seemed that I wouldn't escape it for much longer.

FIRST ARREST AND THE MINERS' DISPUTE

They say you never forget your first arrest, and this is true. There are aspects of mine that I remember, but because I was partnered with Roofer Bob for the first few months I have actually forgotten almost everything else, as you do with bad memories. But I do remember it was a hot day when Bob and I brought a man into the cell block at Radford Road police station, swearing and generally being very uncivil, though our prisoner hardly said a word. There was little conversation with him, as Bob had virtually dragged him from behind the wheel of a car. He then said to me:

"You nick 'im."

"What for?" I replied.

"He's DQ. Nick him."

I assumed correctly that he was disqualified from driving, so I formally arrested him, and then cautioned him, in the correct manner. He must have thought I'd swallowed a police training manual. The man allowed me to handcuff him quite easily, which I was surprised about. I was always surprised when this happened. Many people would allow themselves to be handcuffed and then constantly moan about the pain.

Instead of standing at the charge desk Bob took the man into an adjoining office where I was given my next task.

"Get his clothes off. He needs strip searching."

I probably looked even more bewildered than usual at this, but it didn't seem a surprise to our prisoner because within seconds he was standing naked in front of us, having thrown his clothes all around the room while chuntering obscenities. I was then given one of the most bizarre instructions I've ever had in my life.

"Look up his arse."

"What?" I couldn't think of anything else to say. If I didn't look confused before this I certainly must have then. Where was this leading?

"Check his arsehole. Bend forwards youth!" To which the man immediately obliged by touching his toes with his feet wide apart and legs straight.

"Go on then..." Bob indicated to me, nodding at the man's rear, which now dominated the tiny room. I remember thinking how white and spotty it was as I leaned my head on one side to get a clear view. Yes, it was a bum hole; I could confirm it was there. What on earth? This man had been brought in for apparently driving when he shouldn't have been, and we were both looking up his bum. I didn't realise we had to do this, they never told us at training school. There definitely weren't any bum gazing lectures at Dishforth, unless I'd been in after-dinner sleep mode when it happened.

It was full summer and I noticed a pungent sweaty bottom aroma, and I thought to myself: *What a shit job.*

"I haven't got nowt," the man said, protesting, turning his head around while still bent forward.

To my horror Bob then produced a box of disposable rubber gloves. He put on a pair and threw me the box, indicating for me to do the same. For a moment I prepared myself for the next stage of unpleasantness. What were we looking for? What could the man possibly be hiding up his bum anyway? Was he a magician? Was he about to pull out a rabbit, a string of knotted handkerchiefs, or a stolen television? I'd never put my fingers up another man's bum before, let alone have a poke around. Bob prized the man's cheeks apart and briefly put his face up close to the gaping hole. He nodded and murmured to himself, and it came with a huge sense of relief when Bob said:

"Right then, get dressed."

We searched his pockets. A lighter, cigarettes, some money, all placed on the desk. I listed everything, none of which came from his bum. The strip search had been reminiscent of the scene in *Lawrence of Arabia* in the Turkish Bey's quarters, with people milling about and walking through the office. Bob knew the man very well. It seemed he was a renowned drug dealer, hence the strip search. Somewhere in the arrest process I wasn't told or didn't hear this crucial bit of information. Thankfully looking up a prisoner's bum was not the usual practice for every arrest.

It was typical of the poor communication that existed between me and my tutor. When you don't get on with someone, maybe due to an early misunderstanding or a personality clash, very often the relationship becomes worse rather than better.

I spent the next ten minutes looking for some relatively new carbon paper for the charge sheets and a bottle of Tippex, just in case. Everything was in triplicate, and so two sheets of carbon paper were essential. Some of the typewriters didn't work very well, either the ink ribbons were too ancient or some of the letters didn't function, or both. I found the correct charge in the summons heading book known as the Book 20 and he was bailed to court. It was the first and last time I looked up a prisoner's bum. If it was ever required again I made sure someone else did it for me.

My diaries contain little in the way of enthusiasm for these first few months of active duty in Hyson Green, and I longed to escape. If someone had contacted me in the latter half of 1984 asking me to leave the UK and join them overseas I would probably have grabbed my passport and ran for the door, never to return. I was desperately unhappy with the job and I was beginning to regret joining.

I was aware that I wasn't learning much, all I seemed to be doing with Bob was driving around placating people and not really sorting anything out properly. In police terminology this is called 'knocking stuff on the head' or 'keeping the lid on'. There's very little job satisfaction and it is very unprofessional. To be fair, this was not entirely Bob's fault. The miners' dispute was raging and Bob and I were often the only two cops available in that part of the city, everyone else had been drafted onto the picket lines. We couldn't afford to get involved in anything or spend quality time investigating crime. I had never done it before, I was never shown how to do it, and so it followed that I hadn't a clue. We constantly drove from one job to the next knocking stuff on the head. This was how I learned policing. A crime report was something you simply filled in and forgot about, with absolutely no investigations whatsoever. I was told to make sure I wrote 'Offender unknown' on the back of the form, even if the offender was known. The victim was placated with some well-rehearsed platitudes and never seen again. I remember one of Bob's survival mottos when dealing with the public was:

"For fuck's sake don't give 'em your name, they'll just keep ringing you up and you'll never get rid of the bastards."

I was making a lot of money. My basic wage of around £400 a month more than doubled. I ate out most nights, shifts permitting, at a *Berni Inn* steakhouse just down the road from where I lived. I worked months with just one occasional rest day between ten exhausting twelve hour shifts. Recruitment had stopped and Nottinghamshire was under siege by flying pickets from all over the country. As the miners' dispute dragged on it seemed to absorb virtually everyone in Nottinghamshire Constabulary, and eventually I was called up for it. By this time they were clearly getting desperate for staff.

Starting at 3am usually meant waiting at the station to be collected, and then being driven all over the county reacting to radio messages or driving to pre-arranged points. The first time I stood in a picket line was at Harworth pit. I linked arms with colleagues who were trying to hold back a large group of miners outside the gates. My initial thoughts were how very real it all was. I don't mean this flippantly, but when you see large groups of men on the television shouting at one another it may look dramatic, but when you are standing amongst them it is entirely different. These were well-built miners, all using very colourful Anglo-Saxon expletives. They pushed heavily against us and I was so close I could smell their breath and see the spittle flying as they shouted past me at the working miners. It was alarming but I didn't fear for my personal safety. I could see they were looking right through me as though I was an inanimate object, rather than a person. I was a living crash barrier to be pushed against and leaned on, nothing more. During the scuffling there were never any personal conversations on a human level between us, but afterwards there could be. I later saw this in the judicial system, when the defence and prosecution chatted amiably until the court was in session and then everything changed.

By the time I was there we were months into the strike and it was becoming very acrimonious. Our job was simply to ensure the working miners were not prevented from getting to work, and to ensure the trucks were allowed to collect the coal. There were serious expressions on the faces of the miners, and of course there would be, they saw their livelihoods at risk and their whole way of life in jeopardy. It was all about the closure of the mines and the future of the industry, and the miners claimed the government were seeking to destroy the British coal industry. This notion was derided at the time, and even denied by the government, but has since proved to be true of course. All the pits have gone.

I had become a member of 'Thatcher's Army', one of 'Thatcher's Bully Boys' as we were variously known. It was only a year since I'd returned from my travels with my long hair, broad mind and a mild antipathy towards the police. I was now paid to be sworn at and pushed around outside a coal mine. It wasn't pleasant, and though occasionally exciting it wasn't what I wanted to do. Thankfully I never came to blows personally with any of the miners and I certainly didn't relish the prospect. Other colleagues were not so lucky.

Frankly most of it was very boring. They say warfare is the same. There were long periods of sitting around in the blue Ford Transit vans eating rubber sandwiches and trading Mars bars for little packets of biscuits. Life in a van consisted of crushing boredom interspersed with a lot of mutual piss-taking, communal flatulence and belching. I don't remember any female officers being involved, mainly because there were very few of them in those days.

I remember standing on the A614 near Worksop at 4am one morning turning cars around that looked like they *might* contain groups of men who *could* be flying pickets. We weren't sure they were, of course, and they denied it, but we still did it and got away with it. On another occasion the van I was in was sent on a rapid response to another pit, Pye Hill 1, near Selston, where the familiar shout went up for "More troops!" We tore through Nottinghamshire with the blue lamp on the roof turning slowly, dodging vehicles and pedestrians, clinging on desperately as the van rolled around bends at high speed. We had two-tone sirens in the vans, but fully laden with a dozen hairy-arsed coppers these vehicles didn't inspire confidence. When we finally arrived nothing was happening, as was so often the case. We parked up and resumed our positions, trying to sleep between the malodorous bodies and foul-mouthed obscenities.

I saw hundreds of cops from all over the country. There were a huge number from London. I'd heard rumours of impropriety surrounding the Met officers, but I didn't witness anything personally. A famous story was of a man in Nottinghamshire admitting to some local cops that he'd been banned from driving. When the PNC stated he wasn't banned the man was adamant and argued that he was. A Met officer had apparently ripped up his licence in front of him and demanded fifty pounds cash by way of an on-the-spot fine.

I was removed quite randomly, a collar number used to fill gaps, and plunged into the dispute for a day or a few days, then sent back to the dark streets of Hyson Green. I wasn't sure which I preferred. More accurate would be to ask which I hated the least. My overwhelming memory of it all is of being constantly tired, and there didn't seem to be an end to it.

It was outrageous that striking miners were trying to prevent other miners from going to work, but it was also quite disgraceful in my opinion how the police were being manipulated nationally by the government to serve their own political aspirations.

In common with all my colleagues, I was accumulating a vast amount of annual leave and time owing. I dreamed of escaping for a while, and suddenly in October I was able to book some leave. I wondered how this was possible. Maybe it was becoming clear the government, our side, would win the dispute, or maybe I was just too inept to be missed. It was probably the latter.

I had no hesitation in deciding where to go. I flew back to Israel, to the cleanliness and anonymity of the Negev desert, back to Kibbutz Be'eri on the fringes of the Gaza Strip.

ANNUAL LEAVE

I drove to Gatwick airport in my 2CV with Frankie Goes to Hollywood and their song *Two Tribes* frequently on the radio. I was beside myself with excitement at returning to my Shangri-La beneath the summer moon, Kibbutz Be'eri. I boarded the *EL Al Israel Airlines* Boeing 747 and couldn't believe I'd escaped the nightmare that was Hyson Green for a peaceful few weeks near Gaza.

Two elderly Jewish ladies were seated next to me on the aircraft and started playing backgammon. They spoke to one another in short bursts with a mix of Yiddish, English and Hebrew. An Orthodox Jewish man sat across the aisle from me, dressed in black with his *peyot,* ringlets of hair hanging over each ear. I remember noting in my diary at the time that I quite envied people who had faith, any faith. If there was a God it would indeed be nice to know that he cared, but sadly I think we are all alone in the universe.

I remembered my way around Israel with reassuring familiarity. I caught an *El Al* bus from the airport to the legendary Central Bus Station in Tel Aviv and found the right place to stand for the Beer Sheva bus, via Sa'ad Junction near Gaza. It was mid-afternoon on 14th October 1984 and still very warm in Israel. As the bus rolled southwards the countryside became increasingly sparse as we headed towards the desert. Astonishingly I don't recall that I warned the kibbutz I was due to arrive, or even whether I asked permission to stay, I just turned up. There were volunteers there that I knew, Paul from South Shields, Chris from Canada, and Hans from Switzerland, so I just slotted back in as though I'd never left.

I made myself known to Jacko and Hezzie, two of the *kibbutzniks* (resident Israelis) I had known well, and I was accepted again. I'd spent two six-month stays at Kibbutz Be'eri and was known to be a good worker. If my reputation had been different then my welcome would no doubt have matched it. I moved into room thirteen in the ghetto (Be'eri's slightly ironic nickname for where the non-Jewish volunteers lived), and put the kettle on. I had little unpacking to do, just a change of clothing, a sketch pad and my diary. I also had a Sony *Walkman* and a dozen cassette tapes, so I sat in the late afternoon sun outside room thirteen with a cup of tea listening to Tchaikovsky's *Romeo & Juliet.* I was home, and I felt a huge sense of relief.

There were twenty-five volunteers living and working on Be'eri at that time. There were quite a few Swedes and Danes of both sexes, and almost all of them were gorgeous. Some occupied room three where Paul and I had once lived. They bought beer by the crate from the kibbutz shop, and played Roger Waters' *The Pros and Cons of Hitch Hik*ing very loudly across the ghetto every afternoon. I remembered my drives around Hyson Green listening to the same music and I felt as though I was on another planet.

As the sun set on my first day back in the Negev Desert, I turned on the radio to hear The Voice of Peace and *Twilight Time*, sung by The Platters, followed by John Lennon's *Give Peace a Chance.* The same nightly songs and the same twilight routine I heard in 1978 on my first stay in Israel at Kibbutz Dafna on the northern border.

After a wonderful breakfast of eggs and toast in the huge communal dining room I borrowed some shorts and went for a run around the kibbutz perimeter. I ran into the desert through the *wadis* and onto the track leading to the old kibbutz. When Be'eri was first built it was constantly shot at from Gaza so the Israelis dismantled it and moved it out of range. The sky was cloudless, and there wasn't a breath of wind. The desert looked spectacular and the many small *wadis* combined to give an illusion I was looking across the hills of Judea in miniature.

I spent the afternoons reading and listening to music while everyone else was working. I was formally Jacko's guest, so I wasn't obliged to work, but this changed after a few days. On my fourth day I was asked how long I was thinking of staying. It would be at least another couple of weeks, so I was politely informed that I needed to work, to earn my keep. I fully understood this, so I volunteered to operate the huge dishwashing machine in the dining room, a job I was familiar with. The *pardes* season (citrus fruit picking) was about to start but there was a problem with my status as a guest, and whether I was insured to work outdoors, so I worked the dishwasher and actually enjoyed it.

It seems odd now that for a few weeks in 1984 through my activities at Be'eri, Nottinghamshire Constabulary effectively subsidised the State of Israel.

On my first Friday night at Be'eri there was a party in the volunteers' club, the *moadon.* A lot of people drank to excess and I spent some time smooching with a German girl called Ulli. I know this because my diary says so, though I have absolutely no recollection of it.

I went for long runs in the desert with my *Walkman,* listening to Led Zeppelin's *Physical Graffiti.* I ran as far as the

Anzac Memorial, a large, incongruous concrete monument four kilometres outside the kibbutz near Gaza, marking the sacrifice of Australian and New Zealand troops in 1917. I gazed across the fence marking the edge of the Gaza Strip, but didn't dare venture inside as I had on dozens of previous occasions. The fence and barbed wire appeared better maintained than before. Maybe the prerequisite level of naivety just wasn't there anymore.

I enjoyed my few hours a day operating the dishwasher and felt relieved that I was making a contribution to the kibbutz, even in a modest way. I remember I spent those few weeks laughing out loud constantly, dumping huge blocks of stress all across the Israeli desert.

Kibbutz life lends itself to deep introspection, so after two weeks I began to ponder what I had back in England. In those days once a cop had passed the first two probationary years, it was highly likely the entire service would be completed. It seemed unlikely that I'd even get through the first year so yet again I had to think about what I wanted to do with my life. Maybe I would return to the kibbutz permanently? I felt very happy living abroad, so perhaps that was the answer, unless something unexpected came along to keep me in the UK.

FOOT PATROL

ON MY OWN

In November I returned to the beautiful surroundings of Epperstone Manor, on a Progress & Monitoring Course. My exam results were improving, and I even gained 99% in a definitions test. There was now a practical application to it all of course, so this clearly helped. The miners' dispute ended with a slow whimper rather than a bang, and cops gradually began returning from the front. We were briefing on sixteen or seventeen uniformed constables at the start of every shift, and finding enough chairs for everyone was a common problem. Something that is particularly noteworthy was the wide cross-section of age and experience on the shift; there were newcomers like myself, but many older veterans still in uniform and enjoying the job. This was to drastically change later when so many different plain-clothes squads were set up to deal with specific problems. These 'squads' sourced the majority of their staff from the uniform front line, which was seen as a bottomless pit of staff. It is still seen as this today, even though the pit is now frighteningly empty most of the time.

With all these cops around there was no longer any excuse to merely 'knock stuff on the head'. Suddenly crimes were something we had to investigate rather than simply file away and forget. I hadn't been shown how to do this properly so it came as a shock. My tutorship, for what it was worth, was now over, so I became a foot beat officer, as I should have been at the start. I walked the streets of Hyson Green and Forest Fields in my smart new uniform feeling like Jacques Clouseau, Peter Sellers' character in the *Pink Panther* films, clueless and naïve. I hadn't really grasped what I was supposed to do. Of course I would attend incidents if I was sent to them via my radio, but other than that I thought my job was to simply wander about looking smart all day long, and sometimes all night.

Due to the vast number of uniformed officers I wasn't sent to many jobs in my early days on foot. At that time each police station of any size had a control room which was usually staffed by members of the same shift and so you were personally known to the call-takers and despatchers. Consequently the experienced response cops were sent to the urgent jobs, leaving the lesser incidents to people like me: jobs such as old ladies reporting a window broken or kids kicking footballs in the street.

Each uniformed shift or 'section' was split into two, and each half had a uniformed sergeant. Each section was governed by its own uniformed inspector. There were five 'sections' of uniformed cops providing twenty-four-hour cover, and a sixth extra section to deal with miscellaneous tasks. In the '80s any plain clothes duties required by uniformed officers were dealt with by the 'six section'. These could be anything from football matches to undercover work, and it was staffed entirely by uniformed cops each taking a turn of a few months on the section. It was a great way to gain experience in other aspects of policing.

Your own inspector knew you very well, both personally and professionally, and he (because in those days it would *not* be a female) would fight for and support his own section.

Other inspectors tried to poach staff from other sections to perform unpleasant or difficult tasks their own staff were reluctant to do, so your inspector was there to protect you, and it worked very well. Each sergeant kept a hand-written work book, like a large ledger, where his staff recorded their daily work. Arrests and summary offences were recorded in neat columns drawn with an ink pen and a ruler. Even verbal warnings issued to members of the public were recorded. There was no quota system, and no minimum amount of work required. You simply made an entry in the book whenever you prosecuted anyone. There should therefore be a steady flow of work from each officer, enough to prove you were earning your pay. There wasn't a lot in the book from me because I was still knocking stuff on the head, and this was where I had my first problem.

My first sergeant, Dave, was ex-CID. His face was creased and leathery from a lifetime of chain smoking. Sometimes when on early shifts he would arrive late and you could find him in the gent's toilets shaving, a damp cigarette balanced precariously on the edge of the sink. His early morning smoker's cough was clearly audible across the whole station. He was very thin and I thought he was extremely old, but he couldn't have been more than fifty.

The other sergeant on three section was Mick and he was the complete opposite to Dave. Mick had glass-shiny shoes, was always prompt, quietly spoken and approachable. He was very smart, didn't smoke and had a fresh, healthy complexion, even if he was a ginger. I wished he was my sergeant. I should have asked, but in those days it was unheard of for anyone to ask for a move.

I'd made a few entries in the work book during my first weeks of solo foot patrol but I wasn't making much of an impression. Apparently you had to impress and work very hard in your first two years and I was doing neither. I'd spoken to a few members of the public and entered 'Verbal Warning' in the work book several times for various things. Other than that I had nothing to show for several months' patrolling, apart from a few reports for undetectable minor crime. I didn't realise that in order to prosecute someone, it was inevitable that you would hurt their feelings, but I was reluctant to do this. I just wanted to be nice to people and not get anyone into trouble. I hadn't yet learnt that as a cop you can still do the job and be nice at the same time.

I've no doubt on reflection Dave was making strong hints but I wasn't listening, until finally one afternoon when he was probably overcome by sheer exasperation he called me into the sergeant's office. I could tell there was something wrong when he shut the door behind me.

"What do you think you're doing?" he said to me, his deep brown eyes becoming huge in their dark sockets.

"What do you mean?" I said, rather pathetically, wondering where this was going.

"What are you doing? You're not doing anything, are you?" he said, answering his own question. The whites of his eyes were veined and slightly yellow from drinking and heavy smoking. I stood motionless, staring ahead, like an errant schoolboy in the headmaster's office. I fiddled with my black leather gloves and began to feel extremely uncomfortable. Dave stepped closer and was only a couple of feet away when he began in earnest:

"You come to work with that gormless fucking expression on your face and you just ponce around doing fuck all!" His voice began to rise in pitch and volume as he spoke. "Well?" I couldn't say anything. Words wouldn't form in my mouth because I didn't know what to say. He was right of course. I wasn't doing anything.

"If you don't get out there and do some work you can take off that uniform and fuck off home!" He continued in this manner for several minutes but after the first few memorable lines my mind began to shut down. I pictured myself back in the Negev desert. They'd be harvesting the citrus fruit now, and the swimming pool would have been closed for winter. This drifting off easily happens when you hear things that you don't want to. Your mind begins to wander. My first thoughts were that Dave's admonishments were clearly loud enough for the whole station to hear. I felt an inch tall by the time he finally ended his tirade with:

"Now fuck off out my sight!"

I don't remember what I did for the rest of the shift. I do know that no-one offered any help or advice of any sort, even though they must have heard everything. I felt incredibly alone. That night after work I sat in my flat with my police epaulettes in my hands, the shiny metal numbers catching the light, and I wept. It was all over.

A few days later I was summoned to see the Divisional Chief Superintendent at B-Division Headquarters in Hucknall. I was formally told that my career was in jeopardy, mainly because I was crap. I stood in my best uniform holding my helmet and white gloves while a red-faced old bloke behind his desk repeated what Dave had said to me, but much more politely.

"Not everyone can be a copper you know. It's a difficult job, and there's no shame in admitting it's not for you. It's certainly not right for everyone."

I had some serious thinking to do. When I finally had the nerve to discuss it with a couple of colleagues, they suggested I get an HO/RT1 book, stop a few vehicles, and issue the drivers with 'producers', in order to generate some work. It was at this time that on reflection I'd reached the point of no return. I thought that maybe I should resign and flee. I had nothing to keep me in England, no ties whatsoever, apart from my parents.

It seemed I'd made a decision overnight while asleep. I'd give it another try. On the next early shift I walked down Radford Road into Basford about a mile from the station, armed with a book of HO/RT 1 forms. These are the Home Office Road Traffic form Number One, issued to drivers in order to produce their documents.

Reigate Road was a short 'rat-run' and it was easy to stand in the road and stop vehicles. A police officer in uniform can demand to see the driving licence of anyone driving a motor vehicle on a road, for no other reason than to check it. This is how drink drivers are sometimes caught; random breath testing already exists using this power. If you stick your head inside the vehicle and smell intoxicants, then a police officer in uniform has the power to demand a specimen of breath. Notice it says 'in uniform'. So I stood in the road, shaking with nervous anticipation.

My first customer was a Ford Transit van driven by a young man a little younger than myself. Two older men were in the cab with him, and all three looked worried. The driver appeared as nervous as I felt and stated he didn't have any documents with him, so I issued him an HO/RT 1. I noted on the tick box form that the vehicle wasn't displaying L-plates.

I stopped other vehicles and realised as I spoke to the drivers that they had no idea how nervous I was. Clearly the whole thing was a bluff, and I was acting when dealing with the public. I learnt the police speak that cops use; a kind of brusque manner that is polite but succinct. There is no other way to conduct yourself; it's all part of the act. You can't ask someone for their licence in a Kenneth Williams 'ooer, matron…' kind of manner, it simply wouldn't work. Neither can you give orders as though you are a sergeant major on a parade ground. It has to be somewhere in the middle, and with a professional dispassionate slant to it.

As I issued the tickets I gained in confidence and my shaky handwriting on the forms gradually improved. It was still only 9am when I resumed from my static traffic duty having issued ten tickets. I remember feeling quite elated as I walked back towards the police station reverently clutching my HO/RT1 book in my gloved hands. I'd forcibly changed something in myself, and I was never the same again.

I repeated the process for the next few days, perfecting my attitude and routine. As I did so that particular rat-run became very quiet during rush hour! After a week the HO/RT1s started to flutter into the station like migrating starlings. Half of them were all in order but the others had offences on them. The drivers had produced their documents at the police station of their choice, and staff at the enquiry counters had written down on the corresponding Form HO/RT2 any offences disclosed and reported the person for summons.

The first one, the young man driving the Transit van, hadn't yet passed his driving test. There weren't any learner plates on the vehicle so he'd therefore committed the offence of driving without a full licence, or failing to comply with the conditions of a Provisional Driving Licence, as it is correctly known. I wondered if his employers knew he didn't have a full licence. I checked the number of the van on the PNC and then rang the company. After some initial reticence the manager stated he was shocked and wasn't aware the lad had been driving the van let alone whether he had a licence. I'll never know if he was telling me the truth, but in this instance it didn't really matter. It seemed the other two men in the van had allowed him to drive without authority. I visited the company and took a witness statement from the management. The young driver was then also reported for the offences of TWOC, Taking Without Consent, and no insurance. All this originated from a random stop in the street.

The traffic offences didn't really grab me, but I found the investigation side of it very interesting. There was real satisfaction in this. The foot patrol aspect of my job was pleasant enough, and I really didn't mind it, but in a very modest way and for the first time I'd been introduced to the rewarding world of investigative policing.

MORE LEAVE AND A NEW SERGEANT

In January 1985 I bought my first house. It was a brand new one-bedroom studio house in Nottingham, and it cost £14,000. Yes, that's right, a house, for fourteen grand. I was thrilled and moved in as soon as it was finished. I bought a cheap, tubular, steel two-seat sofa and some crockery but little else. I didn't have a bed of any sort because I was still happy sleeping on the floor. Just before the end of the miners' dispute at the beginning of March 1985 I returned to Israel for a week's leave. This time I took my parents.

We stayed at the Park Hotel near the American Embassy on the seafront in Tel Aviv and rented a car. I took them on a guided tour of Israel they would never forget. We drove north to Kiryat Shmona and then turned right to Kibbutz Dafna. I showed them the kibbutz I'd lived at in 1978 and then we headed up into the Golan hills. We were turned back by a group of rather bemused and heavily armed Israeli soldiers near the summit of Mount Hermon so we pulled over to a small coffee shop by the road. Mist and low cloud from the mountain drifted around the remote stone building and rather optimistically we sat outside at a small and very rusty tin table. Two Arab gents were arguing over a game of backgammon and eventually served us our Turkish coffee in small glass tumblers, which I managed to order in Arabic. They made little comment about our presence, even though we were probably the first strangers they'd seen in weeks. We then drove past the mine fields of the Golan back to Kiryat Shmona and from there to the Dead Sea.

We climbed Masada, the spectacular flat-topped mountain that was once King Herod's palace. The sun was setting as we reached the top, and the Judean hills appeared barren and a wonderful ochre colour in the calm evening. I later described Masada in one of my other books; suffice to say it is an incredible place. The next day we drove through the West Bank. We passed a very large bullet-riddled steel sign by the road which read in Arabic, Hebrew and English: 'Entering the West Bank: Proceed at your own risk'. We stopped in Jericho to buy fruit from a roadside stall, the location of which was in the news the following week when it was blown up by a bomb.

Jerusalem was incredibly interesting as always, and I bought more souvenirs from Arabs in the Muslim Quarter. South in the Negev desert near Gaza my parents were shocked at the Spartan conditions I'd happily lived in at Kibbutz Be'eri in 1982. We ate in the communal dining room and I decided then to stay for a few days and re-join my parents in Tel Aviv to fly home with them at the end of the week.

Back in the real world I continued to immerse myself in my work. Each officer in the station had a pigeon hole used for storage of mail and paperwork, known as a docket. Mine began filling up. In those days the station was periodically given handfuls of pro-forma witness statements from the electricity board reporting domestic pre-payment meters broken into and the cash contents stolen. These were known colloquially as 'meter breaks'. On the majority of occasions the occupants of the house were not surprised to see the police at their door and rarely offered any resistance. It was clear the man from the electricity board noticed the meter had been tampered with when he read it, and would report it to the police, so it was only a matter of time.

Meter breaks were an excellent way to learn the process of arrest, interview and charge. What became evident to me was that most households caught breaking into their electricity meter often had common problems; the house was filthy, the kids scruffy, there were partially completed DIY projects everywhere, and there was a sad, desperate atmosphere. The average amount of cash stolen from a meter was about £45 and on almost every occasion the explanation given was: 'We needed the money'. I became so relaxed about the procedure that very often I would attend these jobs on my own, when we were expected to make such planned arrests in pairs. I rarely encountered any trouble. The meter breaks continued for years before cash was eventually replaced with top-up cards.

I was becoming increasingly confident and productive, and the work book under my name was one of the busiest. It was around this time that my relationship with my first sergeant, Dave, seemed to recover from the low point of several months before. One night after work at 10pm he virtually ordered me to follow him in my own car to an old pub in Hyson Green called The Smiths Arms. The two of us leaned against the public bar, Dave chain smoking and quaffing pints like it was the world's end. He told me serious tales of policing usually punctuated with many colourful four-letter words, and his usual moribund expression lit up as he reminisced about the great days in the CID. When other customers entered the pub he seemed to know them as though they'd been his friend for years. Some would refer to him by his first name, then others would be very deferential and nod their heads with: "Hello Mr Greasley" and speak to him surreptitiously for a few moments before moving away with their drink. I nodded appreciatively and tried to remember the best bits of what he was saying to me.

I felt honoured to have been invited into this shadowy world as though I was in the presence of DI Jack Regan himself, from *The Sweeney*. I was also desperately trying to keep pace with the drinking. We were wearing our uniforms but with a 'civvie' coat over the top, which was soon discarded after the first few pints. We were then joined by other members of the shift, and then at midnight by the 4/12 shift, until there were probably a dozen cops in the pub, all in uniform. I tend to lose count of how much I drink after about eight pints, and so I did that night. Several hours later we all staggered to our cars and drove home.

Dave retired, or left Radford Road, I don't quite remember which, and a new sergeant came my way. Colin was also close to retirement and was a gentle, softly spoken man with a quiet but keen sense of humour. He examined the work book with me and was astonished at the amount I'd accumulated and how much was unfinished. Crime-related matters were neatly finalised but all other things I'd been asked to deal with such as mundane road traffic accidents and similar jobs were quite frankly in a terrible mess, and I knew it. When a piece of work sits in your docket for so long and reaches a certain age, it becomes almost too embarrassing to sort out. That's when the 'dark hole' comes in. It's nothing to do with bottoms, but it's equally embarrassing. Cops have an unhealthy talent for finding places in which to hide or dispose of work that has aged beyond redemption. I later realised that quite a lot of other things in the police could also disappear if they didn't suit. Colin found my dark hole and he wasn't impressed. It may also have been a reflection of Dave's supervision. He'd been ex-CID so I'd had enough support when it came to crime, but he didn't know one end of an accident report card from the other.

"You've got to get rid of all this shit, or you'll end up in the shit yourself..." Colin said to me earnestly, without an ounce of vitriol in his voice. For the next couple of days we sat together sifting through everything in great detail. Much of it was thrown into the bin, but the majority was written off in many imaginative ways until it had all gone. For the first time since being posted there I had a clear docket. I was still in my probation so I couldn't afford to keep my dark hole, and I wasn't expert enough yet to judge what I could ditch and what needed finalising. Colin was a great help and I got on with him very well. Like anyone at or approaching middle age he seemed ancient, as did all the other veteran cops who ambled slowly around the station in their characteristically unhurried demeanour.

All the urgent jobs were given to the young cops like me, as we were keen to impress and learn the trade. The tradition at that time was that you learnt your craft on foot for the first few years before being sent on a driving course, which for me was still somewhere in the future.

We were allowed in the station for forty-five minutes halfway through the shift for a meal break and a game of snooker, but then you had to be out on patrol until ten minutes before the end of the shift. If your inspector found you inside the station without a reasonable excuse you were in serious trouble and were ordered outside immediately. An inspector's authority was never questioned, even for a moment.

I remember one very cold night on foot patrol in the Forest Fields area of Nottingham killing time before I was allowed back in the station. It was snowing hard and I positioned myself inside a covered jitty between rows of terraced houses in Burford Road. Snow whipped around the streets and into the narrow alley where I was standing, but I was quite comfortable in my long black overcoat, thick scarf and huge collar turned up fully around my face. Underneath I was wearing my neatly pressed tunic, a woolly pullover, a long-sleeved pale blue police shirt and clip-on tie, with a thermal vest underneath. Huge snowflakes blew into the jitty on the icy wind and settled on my greatcoat and helmet. The outer layers of my uniform must have been very cold because after a short time I was almost completely covered. It was 4am and all was quiet. Just as I considered moving on, a man stepped into the jitty from the street and collided with me. I didn't hear him approach and he certainly didn't know I was there.

"Jesus Christ!" he shouted, "What the..!" and I'm sure he would have shouted other expletives had I been someone else. He shook his head and without any further comment took out his keys and stepped inside the house on my right. I wasn't even offered a cup of tea!

At 5am I wandered through the waking snowy streets to Beardsmore's newsagents, a hundred yards down the road from the police station. A colleague, Phil, was already there, sipping tea and chatting to John, the proprietor. I was handed a large mug of hot tea which I was very grateful for, while Phil and I leafed through the newspapers on the counter drinking and chatting to John. This was the usual routine before the end of a night shift, providing you weren't inside dealing with arrests or trying to complete urgent paperwork. Despite submitting a form detailing night shifts and rest days, this information was frequently ignored, causing a break in the shifts to attend court, a situation which remains today.

The shift pattern was not conducive to good health and was backward rotating; this meant finishing a week of nights at 6am on a Monday, then back at work at 2pm on Thursday after only three rest days. By Saturday you were at work for 6am, the opposite end of the clock from Monday and only five days apart. This particular early start was frequently 'blobbed', when cops turned up late for work. It was not surprising.

'Tea spots' as they were known, were highly prized and cultivated wherever you could find them. They usually consisted of anyone willing to make a hot drink for a police officer. They were often commercial premises, but occasionally a private individual was ideal. They served an operational purpose too, because frequently your host would tell you important local information without realising they were actually passing on intelligence. Sometimes a tea spot could develop into a lasting relationship. In the latter years of my service I knew an Irishman on my beat area who I visited at least once a week, spending an hour with him in his flat watching TV and sipping coffee. He knew in detail everyone's movements in the vicinity and his flat was ideally located with windows at the front and rear from which I could observe activity. As his health deteriorated I regularly took him his shopping after work, which he paid me for and which mainly consisted of eighteen cans of *John Smith's*. He died a week after I retired.

There was an ancient red brick factory at the rear of Radford Road police station called Hicking Pentecost where there was a night watchman who was always happy to make tea for police officers. He also had a vast collection of dirty magazines, the ladies in the photographs having their modesty covered with black pointy blobs. We often called in at a transport café in the Bobbersmill area of Nottingham called The Mill Café, usually very early in the morning. I remember wondering whether I could ask for the fat to be cut off my bacon, but I never did have the courage speak up.

In the summer of 1985 the 'Live Aid' concert took place at Wembley, and I took part in a sponsored run around Wollaton Park in Nottingham. I held a party in my tiny house on the day of Live Aid with a mix of friends from Dishforth, Radford Road and my travelling days. It was strange to see people from such vastly different chapters of my life together in one place. It was interesting to be in the presence of my new and old self. The two were clearly very different people. I was becoming reasonably good at playing policeman, and it seemed I was starting to enjoy it at last.

DEAD PEOPLE

It was a particularly hot day when I was sent to my first 'sudden death'. The fire brigade had been called to the living room of a ground floor flat on St Paul's Terrace in the centre of Hyson Green. A member of the public had seen what appeared to be thick black smoke through dirty net curtains and there was no reply at the door from the elderly male resident. I wasn't told much over my radio other than the fire brigade was requesting police attendance. I was just around the corner so I volunteered. When I arrived the fire engine was parked directly outside the address. The fire crew were very relaxed and in the process of packing away their equipment. I couldn't see any sign of smoke or water spillage, so I wondered what they'd been doing. As I approached one of the fire officers just pointed to the front door of the flat, which had been forced open and said:

"In there, mate."

I pushed open the remains of the splintered wooden door and stepped inside. The first thing that became apparent was the smell. A surge of foul odour swept over me, gripping my throat, a rancid smell like rotting meat. I opened the door into the front room and it was thick with flies. The insects were so numerous they moved around like a dense cloud of smoke. In an armchair in the centre of the room, facing a tiny portable television was a large, elderly gent, sitting motionless. His hands were resting on the chair arms, his legs were crossed and he was wearing slippers. His balding head was tilted back at thirty degrees on the high-backed chair. His mouth was wide open, and curiously I noticed he didn't have any teeth.

The visible skin on his face, arms and hands, was an olive green like the colour I'd painted so many *Airfix* models when I was a kid. The cloud of flies buzzed in and out his gaping mouth and I tried in vain to keep them away but there were just too many. There were no signs of a struggle, and the poor chap seemed peaceful enough, despite being food for so many insects. I thought at first that he was very fat until I realised that much of his size was due to putrefaction of his body as it had swollen like a balloon. It was full summer and he'd obviously been dead for days or even weeks. The doors and windows had been secure and I confirmed the fire crew had forced entry. I searched through some papers for a name and contact details of relatives. I told the control staff it was a 1/1, a dead body, and after a few minutes a couple of CID officers arrived. The three of us examined the body as it was, and a doctor attended to formally pronounce life extinct. There were no suspicious circumstances, so that was the end of the matter. He was removed to a mortuary and the flat was boarded up. I managed to trace an elderly sister and obtained enough information for a Sudden Death Report for the coroner, which was sent later that day via teleprinter message.

Such calls are quite a routine occurrence but they are all distinctly different. Often the person is not deceased at all, and sometimes not even in the building. A concerned neighbour could have contacted the police thinking the occupant was ill in bed but in reality they'd gone shopping or even away on holiday.

On one occasion I forced the back door to a particularly dark terraced house to find the kitchen floor completely obscured by buckets full of disgusting brown matter. Leading on from the kitchen there were similar containers covering the living room floor, on tables and shelves. Plastic buckets, metal buckets, watering cans, jam jars, cups, glasses, even yoghurt pots full of the same fetid matter. On closer inspection I could see the contents appeared to be human faeces and urine. There must have been hundreds of gallons of it. All around the room there were newspapers and other items piled high to the ceiling, and it was extremely difficult to navigate a path through the house as a result. The smell was such that I haven't forgotten it to this day, as though the proceeds of a huge sewage works were trapped inside a small, airless house.

In an upstairs room I found an elderly man lying fully clothed on a double bed. He was barely alive and clearly had serious breathing problems. His hair was beyond his waist, and at first I thought he had something clasped in each hand until I realised his finger nails had grown so long that they'd rolled around and curled up on themselves like the claws of a big cat. His great bushy beard was matted with rotting food remnants, as were areas of his clothing. It was clear the man was suffering some sort of mental as well as physical illness, but it wasn't until the ambulance arrived that I found out what it was. The famous aviator Howard Hughes had the same complaint in the latter part of his life, and the ambulance crew said it was surprisingly common. It was Diogenes Syndrome, and it meant the sufferer couldn't bear to throw anything away, including their own waste.

One aspect of sudden deaths is delivering the death message. In the days before the internet and mobile phones these were quite common. A relative had died somewhere in the world and it was our job to inform the family. It was Christmas morning when I knocked on a door in Hyson Green, feeling like the grim reaper. A sixty-two year old woman had passed away unexpectedly and so I knew the shock would be total. The door was opened by a smiling woman in her mid-thirties, wiping her hands on a tea-towel. I could smell the turkey, gravy and sprouts boiling in a pan.

"Sorry I'm in a bit of a mess, officer, I'm in the middle of cooking the Christmas dinner, I've got my mum coming round soon."

No you haven't, I thought to myself, just before I told her the bad news.

I attended an address in the Sherwood Rise area of Nottingham later that same year following a call from a concerned neighbour. The tenant underneath had contacted the police after hearing some loud banging and desperate pleading shouts from the flat above. It was at the top of a tenement dwelling and I entered the scruffy bedsit by kicking the door repeatedly. Forcing doors to arrest someone or to preserve life and property was another practical skill we were not trained to do, yet it's something you see cops doing frequently on the television. The door took several of my best kicks before it finally gave in. It had been locked and bolted from the inside. I was utterly shocked by what I found. Everywhere I looked blood was spattered across the walls in great sweeping arcs and occasional star patterns on the ceiling, as though from gunshots. There was one person in the flat, a painfully thin man in his early fifties lying face down on the filthy floor, with a dark pool of congealed blood surrounding his head.

Small clumps of red matter like bits of sponge lay around the room and it all looked very suspicious. *This must be a murder*, I thought to myself. But the flat was on the top floor, there was no fire escape, I'd just forced entry and it had been bolted from the inside. The key was still in the lock, but furniture had been tipped over in a clear sign of a struggle. The man was very definitely dead, but as far as I could see there weren't any injuries to his body, apart from the blood coming from his mouth. What on earth had happened?

I called for another officer, and very soon afterwards two CID officers arrived. We discussed taping off the room for forensic examination, convinced at that point it was a murder scene. When the ambulance crew arrived I immediately noticed how calm they were. They confirmed that he was deceased and then spent quite a long time looking in his mouth and examining the lumpy bits of red dotted around the room. They read the labels on some bottles of tablets and then rolled him over to examine him in detail. There weren't any injuries anywhere on his body.

"On his own was he when you found him?" one of them said to me.

"Yes, yes he was."

"The room was locked from the inside?"

"Yes," I replied, "and bolted." The ambulance crew then chatted briefly to one another, each nodding and commenting before they both turned to us. One of them then said:

"We can't be a hundred percent certain, not until a doctor's confirmed it, but we think he's coughed up a lung, and it's killed him, as it would. I've seen it before..."

KARMA

Of course it isn't usually dead people that hurt you, but the living. I've probably wrestled with hundreds of people in my service, all part of the job as a front line cop. Sometimes people do not want to co-operate with the police, right from the initial encounter, and you end up rolling around in the gutter with them, fighting. You can guess very quickly when this is about to happen because the best warning sign is when they tell you to "Fuck off." In the early days of my service this would send me into a mild panic, thinking back to training school when I failed to subdue the pretend drunk. Later in my service I just sighed and got on with it in the most appropriate manner fitting the circumstances. 'Controlled aggression' as it is known, was something I had to learn, and it was difficult for an ex-hippy like me. Clenched fists, threats, staring eyes and a fighting stance are the other signals that follow. By this time you should have your handcuffs poised at the ready.

I clearly remember the first occasion I dealt with an angry drunken man on my own. I was on foot patrol at 2am in the Basford area of Nottingham when I was sent to a domestic dispute at a terraced house in Suez Street. On my arrival I noticed the front living room window was smashed, and I remember thinking it must have made a lot of noise. I stepped into the kitchen at the side of the house. A thin woman of about thirty years of age with long black hair was standing at the sink crying. She looked up at me.

"You're not on your own are you?" she said as she tried to look behind me. This wasn't a good sign.

"Yes, I am, why?"

"Well it's okay anyway; I think he's gone. He's smashed my window, have you seen it?"

I nodded and took out my pocket book. I'd just started writing notes when I heard footsteps outside coming towards the door. I saw a large figure fill the doorway briefly before it disappeared.

"That's him!" she shouted at me, before turning back to the sink to resume her crying. I stuffed my notebook into my tunic pocket and followed the figure into the street. I saw a man with his back to me walking away, twenty yards down the road, so I shouted:

"Excuse me, can I have a word with you a minute?" and he stopped and turned around. He paused then started walking towards me. As he grew closer I could see he was extremely thick-set with no neck and huge hands like shovels. He was greasy, scruffy and enormous. He looked like one of the morlocks from the 1960 film *The Time Machine,* but the morlocks were much better looking.

"I just want a quick word with you, if that's alright?" I heard my voice sound a little pleading as I assessed the sheer size of the man. He wasn't taller than me, in fact he was a few inches shorter, but as he waddled drunkenly up to me it seemed he took up the entire width of the pavement. A smile spread across his face as he stopped a few feet from me and he simply said:

"What?"

"She tells me you smashed her window?" I said, indicating towards the house and large shards of glass in front of the window. "Is that right?"

"What if I 'ave. What are *you* gonna do about it?"

"I need to talk to you about it down at the station…" I said to him in as informal a manner as I could, doing my best to avoid confrontation. He smiled again, a slow mischievous grin like a Bond villain. In fact he also looked a lot like Oddjob, the oriental gent with the lethal bowler hat in the film *Goldfinger.* I pressed the yellow transmit button on my radio and requested transport. I didn't at that time ask for any formal assistance, but perhaps I should have done. While still staring in my direction he gave me a very calm reply.

"Fuck off."

He then turned around and started walking away. I took out my chain link handcuffs and grabbed his left arm. He seemed quite relaxed so I quickly searched for an exposed area of wrist. I thought I might be able to manage the situation if I could apply handcuffs, and until that moment it was going well. Then to my horror I realised his wrist was as thick as a man's leg, and therefore the cuff wouldn't fit, it was just too narrow. There was absolutely no point trying to handcuff this man. I knew exactly what to do next, so in a flash I pressed the transmit button and sent one word across the airwaves:

"Assistance!"

I heard some replies but by then I was too busy to acknowledge anything. If this man were to get his hands free he would probably pummel me to death in the street. I took hold of both his wrists over his coat and I held on to him as though my life depended on it, which it probably did.

"Get off me, now! Get your fuckin' hands off me!" he shouted. I was close enough to smell his lager breath mixed with stale cigarettes. I could see a moonscape of craters in his pock-marked face and wondered for an instant if this ugliness might be the last thing I ever saw. Several very long minutes passed with me still gripping each arm by the wrists. As if to confirm my suspicions he then started shouting:

"When I get my hands free I'm gonna fuckin' kill you, you fuckin' bastard! You're dead!"

We were moving around in the street, onto the footpath, then back onto the road, as though taking part in a strange ritual dance. The only alternative, as I saw it, was to release my grip and reach for the bit of wood that was wobbling around inside my right trouser leg. But it was whether I could get hold of it in time. I didn't have anything else to use and no other option but to let him go, but this was unthinkable. Don't get me wrong, I dearly wanted to run away, but duty kept me firmly in place. The same sense of duty that kept the men in the Flanders trenches a hundred years ago.

The man's eyes were focussed on some point in the infinite distance, the way drunken people do, and he was snarling like a rabid dog. His face was contorted as though he was in a gurning competition, which if he'd entered at that moment he would have certainly won.

Suddenly at the end of the street I saw a police car pause briefly, the small and ineffective blue lamp on the roof slowly rotating. But they couldn't get to me because of the recent installation of 'tank trap' restrictions in the road designed to stop all vehicles except fire engines. The police car disappeared and with it went any help I was hoping for. It was at that moment I realised just how tightly I was gripping the wrists of this awful man. I heard the sound of ripping fabric as the sleeves of his nylon coat came away at the shoulder, both at the same time, like in a slapstick movie.

The stitching burst to reveal fluffy white filling, and suddenly he was wearing a waistcoat. For a moment we both noticed this and it seemed to piss him off even more, the fact I'd now damaged his precious but very shitty coat.

Another long minute passed before two colleagues pulled up in a police car. A sergeant, John, took hold of the man from behind while Paul opened the back door of the Ford Escort. Paul then grabbed him so I could finally release my grip.

It took three of us almost ten minutes to get this man into the back of the vehicle. He was kicking, throwing punches, shouting and screaming. Paul and I had to sit on top of him in the rear passenger foot well while John drove the car a mile back to the station. He struggled continually and shouted threats and obscenities. As is customary with such violent people he was thrown straight into a cell to calm down. All three of us sustained injuries from this incident. Those were the days before CS spray or Taser guns.

The man's idiot girlfriend later dropped the complaint of criminal damage, and instead we had to merely pursue a charge of threatening behaviour. In the next few days I made enquiries in the street and traced three people who'd witnessed events, two elderly ladies and an inoffensive, quietly spoken middle-aged man. Sadly when their names were disclosed to the defence, as is the custom, the horrible man threatened them. He barged into the man's house, grabbed him around the throat shouting:

"You're not gonna get to court 'cos I'm gonna take your knee caps off before you get there."

I had a desperately pleading phone call from the poor

man wanting to withdraw his statement. He wouldn't tell me why until I visited him and he finally told me what had happened. I could imagine how he felt, and I didn't blame him for it. The two ladies were equally terrified. He'd said to one of them:

"If you go to court and give evidence against me I'll knock you down and piss all over you."

Needless to say this annoyed me deeply. These witnesses were crucial. In a broader capacity the police rely on the public, they can't do their job without them.

I revisited all three of the witnesses and gave assurances regarding their safety. All three were terrified. After much persuasion they finally relented and I obtained additional witness statements describing the threats he'd made. The idiot had stepped up the trouble he was in tenfold, though he didn't know it yet.

As soon as I had the evidence I drove across the city to his address with several colleagues. I arrested him for the offence of attempting to pervert the course of justice. I recorded the interview on hand-written contemporaneous notes, as was the custom at the time. He simply replied, "No comment" throughout the entire thirty-five minute interview. He was remanded in custody. The original offence of threatening behaviour was dropped.

The courts take a very dim view of justice being perverted in this way. He was sent to prison for a year. This was the first time I really felt completely immersed in a case, and it was what is generally known in the police as 'a good job'.

A few months after his release I chanced upon a teleprinter message in Radford Road control room detailing a serious road accident. The same obnoxious man had been

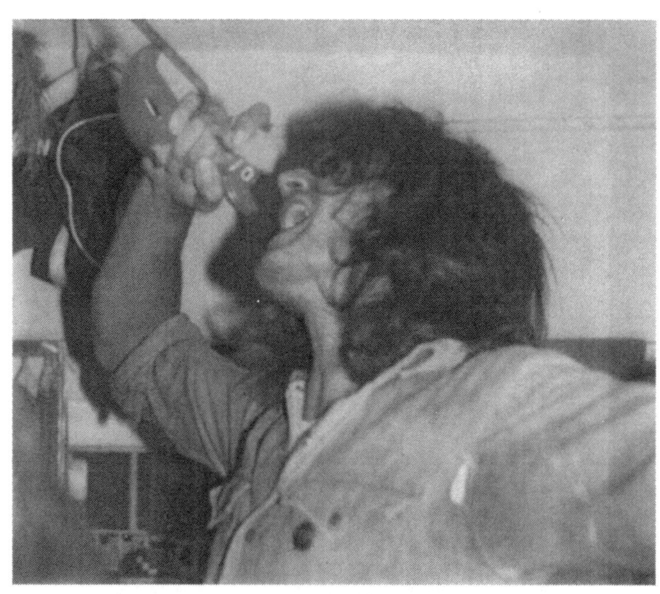

Singing *Stairway to Heaven* using a duck as a microphone, Kibbutz Be'eri, Israel, 1981

A long-haired scruffy hippy.

RAF Dishforth, not taking the job seriously enough.

My colleague, Ted, even less so.

Passing Out Parade, RAF Dishforth, June 1984

With a proud mum on Passing Out day.

NOTTINGHAMSHIRE CONSTABULARY

Radford Road Sub-Division

Nottinghamshire Constabulary is divided into four divisions - 'A', 'B', 'C' and 'D'. Each Division has three Sub-Divisions and Radford Road is part of 'B' Division which has its headquarters in Hucknall. The Sub-Division serves a population of over 70,000 in an area which includes an inner city district and some large council housing estates. There is also a Police Station at Broxtowe, from which a section of Police Officers operate within Radford Road Sub-Division

Based at Radford Road are uniformed and CID officers, civilian support staff and traffic wardens. Assistance is also provided by members of the Special Constabulary. The overall officer in charge of the Sub-Division is a Superintendent with a Chief Inspector as his Deputy.

RADFORD ROAD POLICE STATION

The site was purchased in 1979 and building commenced in 1982. It was completed in June 1984 and occupied the following month, being fully operational within three weeks. The Station was opened officially by Her Royal Highness The Duchess of Gloucester on 21st November 1985. The Police Station is manned continually throughout each 24-hour period.

The fortress where I started and ended my illustrious career.

Nottingham City Centre, 12th May 1986. Moustache, bulled boots, tunic and Burndept radio.

RADFORD ROAD SUB DIVISION

DATE: 6 August 1989			DAY: SUNDAY		6.8.89	RECEPTION
SHIFT	6am - 2pm	8am - 4pm	10am - 6pm	2pm - 10pm	10pm - 6am	WC - RD
SECTION	4B	4A	-	5A/B	3A/B	SH - 4.12 8.4
INSP.	Hucknall	MS		6/2 66	Hucknall	JH - A/L
CUST. SGT	~~698~~ 1435			1581	405	
CONTROL ROOM	JP 1896 16 RS			~~552~~ 43 1769 ~~YG~~	512 1614 MR LR 4112 TL	BROX OFFICE
RAD/RD SGTS	~~1435~~ 698	1358		1274	915 PW106	MO - RD
BROX SGTS		9/5 1016		~~5/4 [illegible]~~		
CONSTABLES RAD ROAD	861 564 1052 1774	~~212~~ ~~218~~ ~~1774~~ 718		~~1897~~ 412 1775 ~~PW169~~ 337 A/L 1604 ~~43~~ PW205 WSC 332 2pm – 6pm	~~1334~~ 1942 478 PW90 881 ~~1959~~ 1087	AREA CONSTABLES
BROXTOWE	~~273~~ 712 1563	~~712~~		814 922	61 1883 1334	PS 309- RD
AREA 1					[illegible] Cones [illegible]	HYSON GREEN 1887- RD
AREA 2					[illegible]	BASFORD SHERWOOD WHITEMOOR 1183- RD*
AREA 3						
AREA 4						F/F 1965 RD* PW 154–sick
AREA 5						ASPLEY 934- RD
AREA 6						BROXTOWE 1288- RD
AREA 7						BEECHDALE BILBOROUGH 1913- RD
AREA 8						
AREA 9						NUTHALL 1692- RD
RESP 1						VEHICLE SERVICING
RESP 2						
RESP 3						

ADDITIONAL OPERATIONAL INFO. Y.G. HOLMES ENQ.

Road Works – Radford Road/North of Wilkinson St crane delivery to Shipstones. 7am to 1pm Road will be closed. Emergency vehicles [illegible] delivery yard on Wilkinson St [illegible] Radford Rd.

Light duties 1896

LION 16 861 1563 66 1769 43 512 66 1334 1883

Typed duty sheets. At the stroke of a pen and some initials you could get the day off.

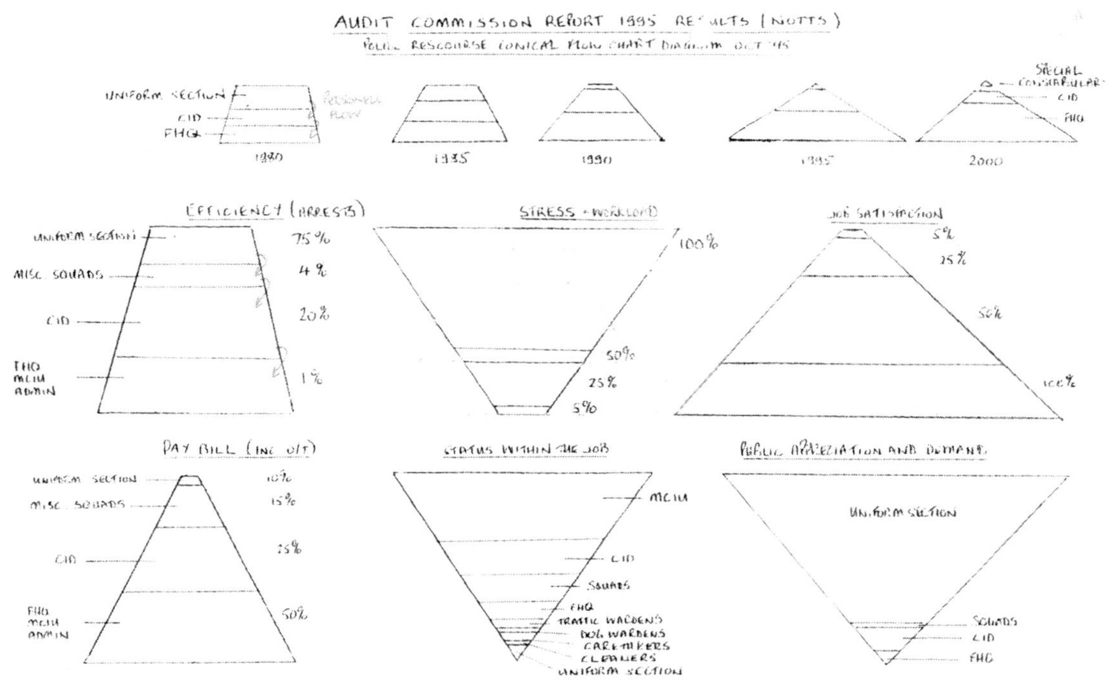
AUDIT COMMISSION REPORT 1995 RESULTS (NOTTS)
UNIFORM SECTION
CID
FHQ
1980
1985
1990
1995
2000
CID
FHQ
EFFICIENCY (ARRESTS)
UNIFORM SECTION
MISC. SQUADS
CID
FHQ
MCIU
ADMIN
75%
4%
20%
1%
STRESS + WORKLOAD
100%
50%
25%
5%
JOB SATISFACTION
5%
25%
50%
100%
PAY BILL (INC O/T)
UNIFORM SECTION
MISC. SQUADS
CID
FHQ
MCIU
ADMIN
10%
15%
25%
50%
STATUS WITHIN THE JOB
MCIU
CID
SQUADS
FHQ
TRAFFIC WARDENS
DOG WARDENS
CARETAKERS
CLEANERS
UNIFORM SECTION
UNIFORM SECTION
SQUADS
CID
FHQ

Injured party did not see/hear anything
No-one else at the address saw/heard anything
No witnesses/suspects known at this time
Nothing stolen/above listed items stolen
None of stolen items identifiably marked/serial no.s n/k
Crime number required for insurance/council
No alarm fitted/Crime prevention advice given to caller
Message tagged for PBO/Night shift/Briefing sheet
Obs passed to Conab/Ch3/UHF Ch35/Details entered on PNC
C7 cycle form completed and submitted
IP asked if they require VCP/Leaflets YES/NO
IP considered vulnerable and VCP/Leaflets to be sent YES/NO
Incident flagged F6 on C&C for letter to be sent

Injured party did not see/hear anything
No-one else at the address saw/heard anything
No witnesses/suspects known at this time
Nothing stolen/above listed items stolen
None of stolen items identifiably marked/serial no.s n/k
Crime number required for insurance/council
No alarm fitted/Crime prevention advice given to caller
Message tagged for PBO/Night shift/Briefing sheet
Obs passed to Conab/Ch3/UHF Ch35/Details entered on PNC
C7 cycle form completed and submitted
IP [illegible]d if they require VCP/Leaflets YES/NO
IP co[illegible]dered vulnerable and VCP/Leaflets to be sent YES/NO
Incident flagged F6 on C&C for letter to be sent

Injured party did not see/hear anything
No-one else at the address saw/heard anything
No witnesses/suspects known at this time
Nothing stolen/above listed items stolen
None of stolen items identifiably marked/serial no.s n/k
Crime number required for insurance/council
No alarm fitted/Crime prevention advice given to caller
Message tagged for PBO/Night shift/Briefing sheet
Obs passed to Conab/Ch3/UHF Ch35/Details entered on PNC
C7 cycle form completed and submitted
IP asked if they require VCP/Leaflets YES/NO
IP considered vulnerable and VCP/Leaflets to be sent YES/NO
Incident flagged F6 on C&C for letter to be sent

Injured party did not see/hear anything
N[illegible]ne else at the address saw/heard anything
N[illegible]tnesses/suspects known at this time
Nothing stolen/above listed items stolen
None of stolen items identifiably marked/serial no.s n/k
Crime number required for insurance/council
No alarm fitted/Crime prevention advice given to caller
Message tagged for PBO/Night shift/Briefing sheet
Obs passed to Conab/Ch3/UHF Ch35/Details entered on PNC
C7 cycle form completed and submitted
IP asked if they require VCP/Leaflets YES/NO
IP considered vulnerable and VCP/Leaflets to be sent YES/NO
Incident flagged F6 on C&C for letter to be sent

Injured party did not see/hear anything
No-one else at the address saw/heard anything
No witnesses/suspects known at this time
Nothing stolen/above listed items stolen
None of stolen items identifiably marked/serial no.s n/k
Crime number required for insurance/council
No alarm fitted/Crime prevention advice given to caller
Message tagged for PBO/Night shift/Briefing sheet
Obs passed to Conab/Ch3/UHF Ch35/Details entered on PNC
C7 cycle form completed and submitted
IP asked if they require VCP/Leaflets YES/NO
IP considered vulnerable and VCP/Leaflets to be sent YES/NO
Incident flagged F6 on C&C for letter to be sent

Injured party did not see/hear anything
No-one else at the address saw/heard anything
No witnesses/suspects known at this time
Nothing stolen/above listed items stolen
None of stolen items identifiably marked/serial no.s n/k
Crime number required for insurance/council
No alarm fitted/Crime prevention advice given to caller
Message tagged for PBO/Night shift/Briefing sheet
Obs passed to Conab/Ch3/UHF Ch35/Details entered on PNC
C7 cycle form completed and submitted
IP asked if they require VCP/Leaflets YES/NO
IP considered vulnerable and VCP/Leaflets to be sent YES/NO
Incident flagged F6 on C&C for letter to be sent

Injured party did not see/hear anything
No-one else at the address saw/heard anything
No witnesses/suspects known at this time
Nothing stolen/above listed items stolen
None of stolen items identifiably marked/serial no.s n/k
Crime number required for insurance/council
No alarm fitted/Crime prevention advice given to caller
Message tagged for PBO/Night shift/Briefing sheet
Obs passed to Conab/Ch3/UHF Ch35/Details entered on PNC
C7 cycle form completed and submitted
IP asked if they require VCP/Leaflets YES/NO
IP considered vulnerable and VCP/Leaflets to be sent YES/NO
Incident flagged F6 on C&C for letter to be sent

Injured party did not see/hear anything
No-one else at the address saw/heard anything
No witnesses/suspects known at this time
Nothing stolen/above listed items stolen
None of stolen items identifiably marked/serial no.s n/k
Crime number required for insurance/council
No alarm fitted/Crime prevention advice given to caller
Message tagged for PBO/Night shift/Briefing sheet
Obs passed to Conab/Ch3/UHF Ch35/Details entered on PNC
C7 cycle form completed and submitted
IP asked if they require VCP/Leaflets YES/NO
IP considered vulnerable and VCP/Leaflets to be sent YES/NO
Incident flagged F6 on C&C for letter to be sent

A page of my additional questions for crime reports, each cut out with scissors and applied with Prittstick.

	1	2	3	4	5
MON	R	2pm/12mnt	7am/5pm	10.30pm/7am	R
TUES	R	2pm/12mnt	7am/5pm	10.30pm/7am	R
WED	7am/5pm	2pm/12mnt	R	1030pm/7am	R
THUR	7am/5pm	R	R	1030pm/7am	2pm/12mnt
FRI	7am/5pm	R	10pm/7am	R	2pm/12mnt
SAT	R	7am/5pm	10.30pm/7am	R	2pm/12mnt
SUN	R	7am/5pm	1030pm/7am	R	2pm/12mnt
Hours	30 hrs	50 hrs	44 hrs	32 hrs	40 hrs

The ten-hour shift system when it first appeared. Seven consecutive night shifts followed by six rest days.

Do you keep falling asleep in meetings ? Here's something to change all of that.

WANK Word BINGO

How to play: Simply tick off 5 WANK Words in one meeting and shout out BINGO!

It's that easy!

SYNERGY	TAKE THAT OFFLINE	STRATEGIC FIT	AT THE END OF THE DAY	GAP ANALYSIS	BEST PRACTICE	THE BOTTOM LINE	TOUCH BASE	LESSONS LEARNT	STRATEGIC
REVISIT	GAME PLAN	BANDWITH	HARDBALL	OUT OF THE LOOP	GO THE EXTRA MILE	BENCHMARK	THE BIG PICTURE	VALUE-ADDED	MOVERS AND SHAKERS
BALL PARK	PROACTIVE, NOT REACTIVE	WIN- WIN SITUATION	THINK OUTSIDE THE BOX	FAST TRACK	RESULT-DRIVEN	EMPOWER EMPLOYEES	NO BLAME	STRETCH THE ENVELOPE	KNOWLEDGE BASE
RESULTS - DRIVEN	TOTAL QUALITY	SLIPPERY SLIDE	TICKS IN BOXES	MINDSET	KNOCK-ON EFFECT	PUT THIS ONE TO BED	FOCUSED	QUALITY-DRIVEN	MOVE THE GOAL POSTS

TESTIMONIALS FROM OTHER PLAYERS:

"I HAD ONLY BEEN IN THE MEETING FOR FIVE MINUTES WHEN I YELLED BINGO."

"MY ATTENTION SPAN AT MEETINGS HAS IMPROVED DRAMATICALLY."

"IT'S A WHEEZE, MEETINGS WILL NEVER BE THE SAME FOR ME AFTER MY FIRST OUTRIGHT WIN."

"THE ATMOSPHERE WAS TENSE AT THE LAST PROCESS WORKSHOP AS 32 OF US LISTENED INTENTLY FOR THE ELUSIVE 5TH."

"THE FACILITATOR WAS GOBSMACKED AS WE ALL SCREAMED BINGO FOR THE 3RD TIME IN 2 HOURS."

"I FEEL THAT THE GAME HAS ENHANCED THE OVERALL QUALITY OF MEETINGS PER SE ON A QUID PRO QUO BASIS."

"PEOPLE ARE NOW EVEN LISTENING TO MUMBLERS, THANKS TO WANK WORDS."

"BONZA! YOU COULD HAVE CUT THE ATMOSPHERE WITH A CRICKET STUMP AS WE WAITED FOR THE 5TH DELIVERY."

RAMADAN AND EID-UL-FITR

The Islamic calendar is a lunar calendar, and months begin when the first crescent of a new moon is sighted. Since the Islamic lunar calendar year is 11 to 12 days shorter than the solar calendar, Ramadan migrates throughout the seasons. For 2013 the period of Ramadan starts around **9th July** continuing until approximately **7th August**. It is followed immediately by the festival of Eid-ul-Fitr.

Ramadan is an extremely important period for Muslims. The fasting during the month is one of the five pillars of the Islamic faith. Eid-ul-Fitr is the main celebration in the year for Muslims.

Staff need to be aware of the increased attendance at Mosques, especially for Friday prayers, which increases the profile of both Muslims and their religious buildings within the wider community.

Muslims continue to be targeted for racist incidents and the likelihood of further acts may well increase during this time. Officers should take this into account when responding to any reported incidents at Mosques.

Staff should also be aware of the restrictions (particularly fasting) so that they are able to recognise the period's significance in their interactions with the Muslim community and, particularly, with their Muslim colleagues. Practical examples of this recognition would be:

- Provision of meals during Ramadan to a detained Muslim at sunrise to allow for fasting during the day and the provision of a meal at sunset to break the fast in accordance with practice.
- The simple courtesy of a greeting such as "Happy Eid" (pronounced 'eed') or "Eid Mubarak" (pronounced 'mo-baa-ruk') to a Muslim person during Eid-ul-Fitr.
- Applying discretion in a similar way to that normally exercised at Christmas and avoiding, where possible, non-urgent planned arrests and enquiries affecting Muslims during the Eid celebrations.

These examples are not comprehensive and staff should always be willing to consider whether there are particular needs affecting a Muslim person during this period.

Some of the special instructions for all staff regarding Ramadan.

At the music club gig with the prison van, Sherwood Festival, summer 2011.

At the community centre.

The Police Review needed someone who looked 'tired and fed up', so I volunteered immediately.

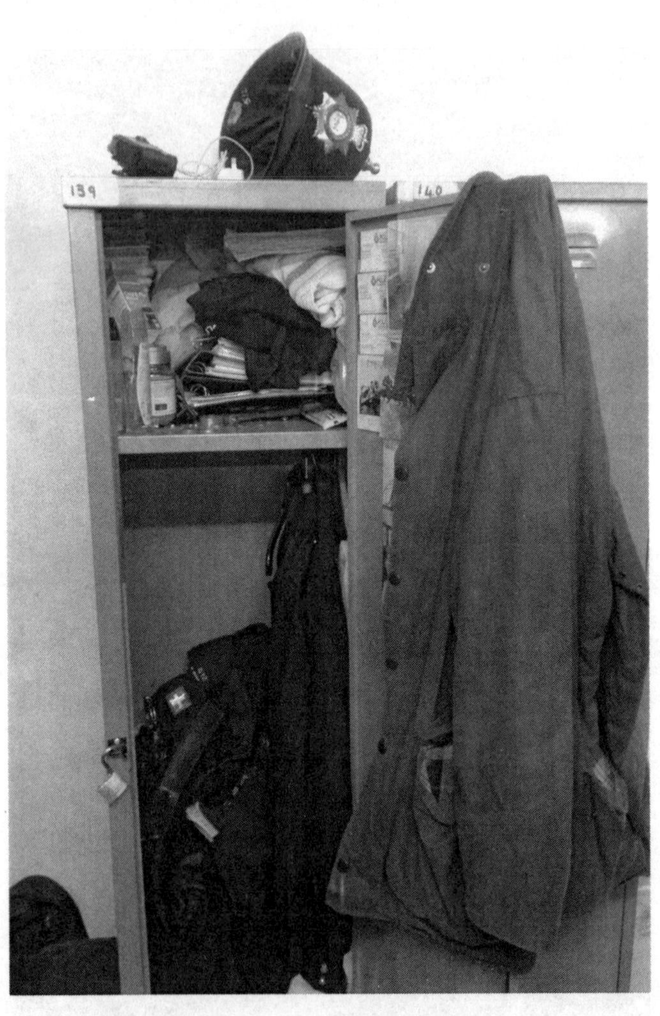

The locker in which everything was meant to be kept neat and tidy.

Late summer 2013 in Hyson Green, Nottingham.
Probably one of the last occasions I wore full uniform.

GETTING STUCK IN

THE FIRST DECENT 'COUGH'

Several important personal events took place towards the end of 1985. The first of these occurred when a colleague threw a party in the Beeston area of Nottingham. I attended with Dave Kato-sideburns, from training school. I left later that night with a phone number given to me by a charming young lady. Unknown to me she'd seen me running through Wollaton Park on the sponsored run weeks before. Six months later Alyson moved into my little house. Her dad, Ron, lashed her wardrobe to the vinyl roof of his beige Austin Princess. Meeting Alyson was a life changing event. It altered my perspective on everything, including the police. We were socialising with other cops and their girlfriends, and thoughts of leaving the country began to evaporate.

In the autumn I attended a two-week residential course at RAF Dishforth, known as the Continuation Course. If you reached this point it was almost certain you would have your probation confirmed. It seemed that I might make it after all.

This was also the time when I converted to a four-seat Cessna 172 at the flying club. I started taking passengers, mainly police colleagues, and we sometimes re-enacted the Dambusters raid over the Derwent Dams. I flew the aircraft at the correct minimum altitudes and complied with all the appropriate rules of the air of course.

The Hyson Green flats complex was a real nightmare to police because the residents knew every possible escape route. I remember walking under one of the elevated walkways hearing a male voice from above saying: "Gob on his helmet." I thought they'd missed until back at the station I found a long trail of phlegm down the back of my tunic. Lone patrolling at night was discouraged and once inside the myriad of walkways you were certainly aware of some personal vulnerability. It was almost a badge of honour therefore to be given Area One, which included the flats.

Late at night it was common for a group of us, usually led by a sergeant or inspector, to visit the complex in order to find the latest West Indian 'blues party'. Sadly this wasn't so that we could all have a smoke and chill out with them, but because the noise was usually audible for hundreds of yards in every direction, and complaints were numerous. Once the source of the loud reggae music was found, a casual approach was used, with hats off and passive body language. We'd usually find dozens of people in the flat, and many were overtly smoking cannabis. They were also found to be selling alcohol illegally, hence the other name for such events, 'shebeen'. In the interests of community cohesion, in other words, fear of causing a riot, such offences were conveniently overlooked at the time. I never encountered any violence or even threats during such visits, but there was plenty of teeth sucking and chuntering. We were The Babylon, and were seen as the oppressors. The person running the event was spoken to, some intelligence gathered, and finally they were asked what time they intended to finish. Then we left. Action was taken at a later date, but it was rightly deemed to be too heavy handed to break it up on the night. It would have been very costly, and frankly we didn't have the staff to do it.

There was a huge central boiler system that blew hot air through ducted vents into each flat which never seemed to be turned off. In summer they were roasting, and in almost all the flats the windows were kept wide open as a result. The interior floors were smooth cement and most tenants had simply painted them to suit, which over time had worn away in places. No doubt these flats and others like them were the results of some progressive '70s thinking, but they looked horrendous to live in. Their reputation was dreadful and further worsened the entire area. There was a large mural in the centre of the complex depicting a man walking on the moon. It was the single best thing about the flats, and totally appropriate.

Early in January 1986 one of the flats' residents visited the police station reporting theft of a CD player. The complainant was described to me as 'a bit of a niff-naff' by staff at the counter, and though rather scruffy looking, and possibly a bit ESN (Educationally Sub Normal), as we used to say, he was far from being a complete snaff. The offender, I was told, lived in Bergholt Walk, and he'd stolen the CD player to raise cash for a drug habit. I thought this could be quite an interesting job, it appeared easily detectable, and so I took a witness statement.

I found the address on Bergholt Walk, stepping around the usual mounds of dog shit and litter in the walkways, and knocked on the door. It opened as I touched it so I walked straight in with a colleague, Tim. Pungent odours of stale tobacco, accumulations of dirt and body odour greeted us in the filthy flat. I shouted "Police!" and heard some scuffling and cupboard doors being banged shut. A thin and very scruffy chap in his mid-thirties with straggly brown hair like rat's tails was standing in the kitchen. I asked him his name and he confirmed he was the man I was looking for. I told him why I was there and to my astonishment he immediately opened a cupboard door and produced the stolen item. Sometimes when the unexpected happens it can throw you off guard a little. I said to him:

"I am arresting you on suspicion of theft and taking you to Radford Road police station where further enquiries will be made." I cautioned him: "You are not obliged to say anything but what you say may be written down and used in evidence." I was so delighted by the quick recovery of the CD player, that I handcuffed him and bundled into the police car straight away. We didn't search him or his flat.

While my prisoner was standing at the charge desk in the station a colleague noticed two small plastic bags of white powder on the floor at his feet. He picked them up and said to my prisoner:

"What's this?" to which he looked blank and replied:

"No idea, never seen it before…"

Tim and I should have searched the man before we put him in the car, or better still, while he was in the flat. The powder was placed in an exhibit bag and handed to me. There were no other detainees in the vicinity, so it seemed likely my chap had tried to rid himself of it.

It was January 1986 and we were only just trying to comply with the new regulations of the Police and Criminal Evidence Act 1984. Though passed in '84 it didn't become effective until the latter part of 1985, and was some of the most influential legislation ever imposed on the police. It completely revolutionised the way a person was dealt with in custody and replaced the nebulous 'Judge's Rules'. Until then the arresting officer had a huge amount of autonomy when dealing with his arrest, and very little accountability. It was commonplace to throw your prisoner in a cell with instructions to think about coughing the job, leaving him there for hours or even all weekend in order to 'soften him up' for interview. I saw prisoners chained to radiators or even bannister rails in old police stations. To be fair, sometimes this was through necessity rather than calculated malice. Many of the buildings such as Gregory Boulevard police station were unfit for purpose. But after being lashed to a hot radiator the detainee would most likely admit anything.

Making sure your prisoner admitted the offence was the most important aspect of an investigation, and there were many interview ploys available. Shouts and threats were common, and some of the older CID officers used the tactic of threatening a prisoner with the arrest of his wife or taking his kids into care if he didn't cough the job. It was all seen as good interviewing in order to put the offender under immense pressure. I was reminded of what one of my first sergeants told me: "Don't worry if you have to bend the rules, you are acting in the interests of justice."

The PACE Act reduced such opportunities dramatically. An admission is still great evidence, but latterly we were told it would no longer be enough to secure a conviction without corroboration such as additional witnesses or forensics. Threats or inducements are no longer permitted, and the promise of bail if the job was coughed could now jeopardise the whole case. Most cops had to completely rethink their interview technique when the PACE Act was introduced. It was seen by many as being too soft on criminals and overly concerned about their welfare. Every moment a person was in custody was now accounted for and recorded on a comprehensive hand-written 'Custody Record'. Before this it might be recorded on the back of the detention report, or 'Domestic Sheet' as it was called, but only if anyone could be bothered.

Cops could no longer interview a drunken prisoner, because quite often they'd admit anything when pissed. If they said they were tired they had to be left in the cell for eight hours so they could get some sleep, which was outrageous. Keeping a prisoner awake until they coughed had always been a great ploy during night shifts. Up until then I had rarely seen anyone ask for legal representation, and if they did, the news flew around the station immediately. Had they committed murder? Why did they want a solicitor? After the introduction of the PACE Act everyone seemed to want one, and the Legal Aid bill grew rapidly as a result. At one point quite recently, Legal Aid was costing almost as much per year as the total funding for all forty-three police forces in England and Wales. The biggest reason of course was that for the first time the detainee was actually asked correctly and given detailed advice about it, crucially having to sign for their decision.

Two hours later I started an interview, recording it on contemporaneous notes. This meant writing down the questions and answers while talking. It was far from ideal, and you had to write quickly to keep a continuous flow. Taped or video interviews were still many years away. My prisoner, now officially known as a detained person, didn't want a solicitor. Even though he had a long record, typical of the time he'd never used one before. The interview went well at first, and he admitted theft of the CD player, but he knew he had no choice. When I took out the white powder his attitude changed. The following is a verbatim extract from the interview notes:

512: Are you taking drugs at the moment?

Reply: I have been for a long time.

512: What do you take?

Reply: Speed. I'm not denying I don't take speed. I take about two grammes a day, 'cos I'm a heavy user of speed.

512: This was found close to where you were standing in the cell block after your arrest. Do you know what it is? (REFERRING TO POLICE EXHIBIT ONE)

Reply: It's some wraps

512: Where did they come from?

Reply: I don't know

512: In your property there's a needle. Has it been used?

Reply: I'm not sure, I wouldn't deny it.

512: Supposing we get the needle and this stuff examined and it turns out to be the same substance that would prove it to be yours wouldn't it? *(This was a complete bluff on my part)*

Reply: Why is that speed in there?

512: You tell me

Reply: You can do all the tests you like, that is not mine

512: Where did this come from then, fall from the sky did it?

Reply: I don't know. It seems like a set up to me.

512: You've said to me already that you're on two grammes of speed a day and then we find this stuff in our cell block right where you were standing.

Reply: Yes alright. It's mine.

This was my very first cough and I was elated. I've absolutely no doubt whatsoever that had this man been given legal representation he would have been advised to answer 'no comment' to all my questions. I would then have been unable to prove the wraps of white powder were his, unless the bags were sent for forensic examination. Because 'speed' or amphetamine sulphate was a Class B drug, and Class 'A' if injected, under the rules of the day I was obliged to contact the drugs squad. Twenty minutes later a detective inspector and a detective police woman (known as a DPW) arrived and took my prisoner from me for a while.

Later I travelled in a plain car with the DPW to my prisoner's flat. We found small weighing scales and some plastic deal bags, and in the kitchen drawer a syringe containing red liquid that looked like blood. We interviewed him again:

DPW: There appears to be blood inside this hypodermic. What is inside it?

Reply: Speed. Amphet.

DPW: Why is it red?

Reply: I was flushing it when you lot banged on the door.

512: Flushing it?

Reply: Yeah. Inject it and pull back the plunger and it fills with blood, then inject it. Flushing.

512: Will you roll your sleeves up for me? *(I noticed numerous puncture marks on the inside of both arms.)*

512: How long have you been using amphetamine?

Reply: About fifteen years.

DPW: Where do you get the syringes and needles?

Reply: From the same people I get the drugs from. Some guy in the pub. Don't know his name.

DPW: How much do you pay for the syringes?

Reply: Two pounds. I bought the rocket (RE-USABLE SYRINGE) for ten pound.

DPW: How much do you pay for the wraps?

Reply: Ten or twelve pounds.

I charged my prisoner with theft and possession of amphetamine sulphate. He was bailed a month hence, to early February. Probably because he was off his face on speed he didn't attend court, so I called around his flat and brought him to the station. I then charged him with his bail offence but this time he was remanded in custody.

I noticed he constantly used expressions such as 'far out', 'bombed', 'tripping' and so on, words and phrases commonly used in the drug sub-culture. It occurred to me that until recently I'd used these expressions myself when I was immersed in the same sub-culture.

TECHNOLOGY AND CARS

In February 1986 my two-year probation was confirmed. It had become a formality by then, as I was enjoying the job and was quite good at it. There was no formal ceremony but I did receive a letter from Fraggle Rock. If I wanted to, I could now make the police my life, at least for the next twenty-eight years until retirement. I understood the significance of it by talking to my peers. They all spoke about their time in the job, but more specifically the years they had left before they could escape into retirement. Cops looked at the finite thirty years almost as a sentence to complete and everyone seemed to be counting down to the end. The amount of service you had was crucial to almost everything, and very often you were judged on that alone. It was also used as a kind of career template. After the first two probationary years you'd get a driving course and work response for a while, then you could specialise in the CID or another department.

There was no official tenure so once in the CID you could call yourself a DC and ditch the uniform for good. I often saw people 'squad hopping' all their service, leaping from one specialist department to another, vanishing for years until they reappeared under a new job title, but still a safe distance away from the uniformed front line. In my humble opinion everyone should spend at least a year on response duties between squads, if only to remind them how lucky they are in escaping.

Getting onto the CID wasn't easy. You needed a few decent arrests which might involve working with CID officers for a while, getting to know them, and crucially, getting to know the DI, the boss. It would also mean buying the detective inspector a drink as often as you could, getting on well with him until he finally uttered those all-important words, "You ought to come and work in the CID, leave it with me I'll have a word with your inspector." The process could take months and involved a lot of drinking.

In the mid-1980s the police didn't have a lot of technology. The control room at the brand new Radford Road police station had two computer terminals, and were the only computers in the entire building. This seems odd now, and almost unbelievable considering the ubiquitous nature of today's technology. It was probably a lot less than most other places at the time too, because the police have always been lamentably late in acquiring new technology. Even when the new systems arrived they were often already hopelessly inappropriate. This could have been due to a cock-up on the procurement front by senior officers with no knowledge of technology, or the misguided belief that technology beats boots on the ground, which it doesn't, or a mixture of both.

There were three operators in a divisional control room such as Radford Road. These were usually two cops and a civilian member of staff. Sometimes it could be one cop and two civilians. They were ordinary civilians too, not 'civvies' dressed to look like cops as they are today. One computer was dedicated to two systems, the Resource Availability System, or RAS as it was known, and the PNC. The person sitting in this seat also had control of 'the pad'. This was where all the hand-written messages were collated for issuing to officers, and it meant that you were effectively in charge of the station and all the available staff. On this person's right was the other computer, the CRS system. This was the local Criminal Record System, and it contained all the names and details of anyone arrested and charged within Nottinghamshire. It was an extremely quick, friendly and very useful system. Both terminals had green screen monitors with a small flashing cursor, very simple by today's standards. Probably because they were so basic they were easy to use and understand. When you charged a person your collar number would appear in page one of the CRS record adjacent to the offence. I found it very satisfying to see my number in such circumstances.

The two computer terminals in the control room were located beside one another a few feet apart on the front desk. Between them was a large control panel inside a sloping wooden cabinet on which were mounted two black Bakelite telephone handsets. These were the instruments of pre-war technology used to communicate with officers on the outside. There were also rows of buttons and switches which operated the various CCTV cameras around the station and the large sliding doors in the back yard. Radford Road was a maximum security police station and had emergency roller shutters over every external door with 'attack lighting' around the building. To date I don't think any of it has ever been used, and probably never will be, since the cells were removed and turned into offices and store rooms. I heard locals describe it as a fortress, and they weren't far wrong. Designed and built in the early '80s there was a clear anticipation such fortifications might be needed. It even had an air-raid siren on a steel tower in the rear car park which has since disappeared.

At the start of every shift after briefing, each officer would walk into the control room and lean on the chest-high wooden casing of the control panel and note down any jobs that needed doing on their designated beat area. The centre of Hyson Green, known as Area One, was thought to be the most demanding beat at the station, and probably the whole force area. It remains so to this day. A decent response cop would probably take five or six jobs from the pad before disappearing out on patrol. An idle cop would maybe take two or three, and even then they might return saying they hadn't been done. In the meantime if anything urgent came in while he or she was working their way through these jobs, they were diverted where necessary.

The 1980s was the beginning of a very busy time for the police. Crime began rising dramatically every year and no-one really knew why, in the same mysterious way it has fallen in recent years.

The *Burndept* radio was eventually replaced in favour of encrypted equipment. It seemed people could listen to police radios, despite the threat that it was illegal to do so if the information was acted upon. At the start of every shift you took a radio from the locked cabinet and signed for it, writing down on the clipboard which radio you had taken. There was a battery tester in the cabinet, and it was vital to make sure you had enough battery life for the whole shift. You really had no idea what sort of day you would have, which of course was the beauty of the job, so you needed a full charge.

The police cars were ordinary vehicles liveried with day-glow stripes and markings. The public perhaps believe that all police vehicles are somehow 'souped up' and have turbo-charged engines but sadly this is not the case. In

February 1987 I was sent on a three-week residential driving course at Epperstone Manor. Every day we had some classroom work during which we were taught how a vehicle behaves on a road under various conditions and at different speeds, particularly when cornering. A vehicle is in a stable condition when it is being driven straight and all the pressures are acting upon it equally, like an aircraft in level flight. When different pressures are applied such as braking, accelerating and cornering, the problems can start and control – or lack of it – becomes an issue.

The driving course mainly consisted of driving one of the marked vehicles around the local countryside with an instructor sitting in the front passenger seat, and two other pupils in the back, taking it in turns. We drove a Ford Escort 1.3 petrol engine saloon, and learnt how to drive to a specific system. This meant observing the speed limits, holding the steering wheel at ten minutes to two, and using the foot brake rather than the gears to control speed. When approaching junctions the clutch was depressed and the appropriate gear selected in order to move off quickly, rather than changing down the gears routinely, as was taught when first learning to drive. It was all about safely 'making progress', and manoeuvres that would probably amount to a fail in your driving test had to be learnt and demonstrated effectively. This included, when overtaking, moving over to the other side of the road if necessary in order to get a clear view ahead. It also meant straightening bends when safe to do so. It all seems quite alarming to passengers when driving your own car! One of the ways this system is learnt is through verbal commentary. It's not easy at first but it greatly increases awareness of hazards ahead, which is of course why it is done.

"Junction coming up on the left, clear. Pedestrian on the right with a dog, it's on a lead so it's safe. Child on a pedal cycle coming up on the left, slowing down just in case, indicating to pass, no oncoming traffic so I can give them a wide berth, nothing in my rear view mirror so it's safe to proceed, just giving them a tap on the audible warning to make sure they know I'm here. Bend coming up to the right, double solid white lines in the centre of the road, now approaching a blind bend, slowing down and preparing to stop in case of an obstruction in the road. Around the bend and the road ahead is clear so it's safe to proceed. Buildings coming up on the left, pedestrian crossing and 30mph sign slowing down..." and so on. Try it next time you drive a car – you'll find it can be quite exhausting.

I passed the course with seventy-two marks. Everyone seemed to get the same mark, which I found very curious. If anyone passed with more than that – even just one or two marks – they were invited to join the traffic department. One of the candidates on my course was awarded seventy-six marks and because he was also known as 'a good lad' he was given a job in the traffic department almost immediately. As far as I recall he spent his entire career there. This was how you moved between departments in those days, and it seems bizarre now, in today's world of politically correct equal opportunities.

The three-week course was known as a 'standard driving course' and you may be surprised to read that we were not taught how to drive faster than the speed limits. This was probably due to the absence of sirens at the time.

Response duties at a busy station should be reserved for younger cops. Driving a very basic manual car around an inner-city area for eight hours or more with a half hour break in the middle – if you were lucky – was very tiring. It often seems relentless and it can also shred the nerves. You are usually the first to arrive at all serious incidents, frequently alone, day or night, most of the time having no idea what to expect at the scene. On several occasions, when on response duties, I woke up in bed shaking my fists at the bedroom wall, rambling and shouting after a particularly busy day.

Gallows humour can develop too, the type of humour that is banned today. Sometimes anything could lighten the mood and relieve stress. I remember one serious domestic incident I attended with a male colleague when we knew at any moment we could be fighting, he whispered into my ear, "What do you think they'd do if we started French kissing now?"

We'd occasionally chase around the city in the cars on night shifts, spraying one another with fire extinguishers, or practicing handbrake turns in the car parks of industrial estates. We didn't have a 'skid pan' so this was an excellent way to understand the dynamics of vehicle control. In the early years, a colleague called Mark said to me as we sped along Gregory Boulevard in our Vauxhall Chevette at 60mph:

"The gears in this are so shit, watch this for a clutch-less gear change," as he rammed the car into gear causing a loud bang and the car to stop immediately. A few years later, on rare occasions of quiet, another colleague, Phil, used to try crossing the city without changing gear at all. It's astonishing to witness a 1.4 diesel engine successfully performing hill starts in fourth gear. A burning clutch is an awful smell, so it meant keeping the windows open, which was an arse in winter.

New recruits were teased endlessly, with strange initiation rituals invented for them. They were often made to take cycling proficiency tests in the back yard of the police station, with such manoeuvres as 'emergency dismount on the move in pursuit of a suspect on foot' and 'saluting an inspector to the left and right' much to the amusement of everyone else in the building, peering into the back yard. There is a near total ban on any of this fun at work nowadays of course.

I had a refresher driving course a few years before I retired which proved to be a very different experience to my initial driving course. Without ever being formally shown how to use the siren or the flashing lights the driving instructor simply shouted that I was to drive the police car at whatever speed I wanted in order to get across the city as quickly as possible. I thought this was rather strange and potentially extremely dangerous because I'd never been formally taught how to drive fast. The instructor probably assumed I'd already had the training. The truth is I'd been unofficially doing it for many years of course, since the early days of driving with one hand or alternate hands while busy pressing the horn, flicking the headlights and changing gear, in the days before sirens.

It is certainly very exciting driving at 80mph on the wrong side of the road in built-up areas, and probably a lot safer now with sirens and both hands on the steering wheel. But is it really necessary to drive at such speeds? It's very stressful and extremely dangerous. I see young cops tearing past schools while children run around at the roadside. Nothing could be urgent enough to risk the lives of pedestrians in this manner. I think some cops believe the lights and sirens act as a force field around the vehicle,

INSIDE AND OUT

In 1988 my section needed someone to operate the control room computers. I was volunteered for the training by my inspector on the basis that I kept a very neat pocket book. This was typical police logic. I knew absolutely nothing about computers. As with any training course it was Monday to Friday office hours, so it was great to live a normal life for two weeks and be at home during weekends with everyone else. The usual Sunday night blues don't normally happen when working round-the-clock shifts. Sunday nights, with the prospect of another working week ahead, could actually fall on any day of the week.

After almost four years of working rotating round-the-clock shifts it became clear there were some advantages to shift work. Days off in the week meant there were few traffic jams and the shops were always quiet. If you've ever worked shifts you will understand this. The down side balances the good points though. On a 4/12 shift unless you keep yourself busy during the day it could seem as though you were simply waiting to go to work, and this is worse on a Friday when the rest of the country finishes for the weekend.

The PNC was the first computer I'd ever used, if you don't include playing *Donkey Kong*. I was very impressed with it, as I had been at training school, but now more so since I understood its capabilities. In around four seconds the PNC could search twenty million vehicle records and tell you who the owner was and where the vehicle lived. I was astonished. There were also millions of names on the system, and of course it was a nationwide database. There were other functions of the PNC but by today's standards it was a very basic system. It was more advanced than Nottinghamshire's own criminal record system, the CRS. This system had a maximum capacity of fifty convictions on any one record. When I was first trained in its use it was extremely rare to find anyone with so many convictions. Sadly as the 1980s progressed it became increasingly common to see records with far more than this. Today criminals have convictions numbering in the *hundreds.* You have to ask yourself, how does someone accrue so many? Surely common sense would suggest the offender is not learning anything from the criminal justice system? Nottinghamshire's own CRS system was eventually scrapped. I suspect it couldn't cope with the amount of offending.

Later the same year I submitted a request to be married, complying with police regulations. My prospective wife and her family were then checked for suitability to marry a police officer. Luckily I was granted permission. I'm not sure what would have happened if it had been refused.

As soon as I returned from my computer course I began working in the control room at Radford Road. At first it was just the occasional shift, but then it was for weeks and eventually several months. This carried on for the next few years, working inside and then outside, then back inside again. I still worked shifts with the same people, and I found the role genuinely interesting. It was very challenging sometimes when working the pad, being in control of the station. Split second decisions had to be made as to who should attend urgent calls from the public, and the stress levels were sometimes very acute.

Because I was tied to my own shift it was an unwritten rule that you didn't usually ask a member of another shift to take jobs off the pad, unless absolutely necessary. There was a pride in your own shift managing to 'keep the lid on' and to clear the pad. This was known as 'cardboard visible' and it was great to hand over to the next shift with nothing waiting, though this was quite rare. On some shifts it was so hectic that you hardly had enough time for a toilet break, and certainly not a meal break, in the whole eight hours. Food was taken at the desk while working, there was no alternative. This was another thing we did in order to make the job work, when perhaps it shouldn't. It was very stressful at times. The RAS computer had a bell, as did the roller shutters to the cell block and the link with the front counter. All these rang in the control room, with the addition of five telephones which never seemed to stop ringing, except for a few hours in the middle of the night. We also had a red telephone on the front desk called The Bat Phone, just like in the TV series. It was a direct link to the main VHF control room at Fraggle Rock, and someone had actually drawn a picture of a bat on it. Add to this the constant radio chatter and some ambient noise from colleagues standing around chatting; it was often loud and unpleasant.

So what happened when a member of the public rang the police? All '999' calls were taken at headquarters and then sent down the line via the RAS computer system. If a caller rang the police station directly on the local number rather than using the 999 system a hand-written message was created by the control room staff. If a member of the public called at the station in person the enquiry counter would write a message for the control room. It hasn't changed much and the same procedures apply today, but now everything is entered directly onto a computer.

Very often it became impossibly busy, to the point where no-one was available to attend calls. When this happened some less urgent jobs were disposed of, or ditched, as we called it, in order to make the job work. They were taken off the pad and placed in 'Docket Thirteen' as it was known: the bin. All incoming messages should have been stamped with a hand-held consecutive numbering machine, but at very busy times this was overlooked. On these occasions 'when the wheel came off' as we called it, even some stamped messages were ditched. If you ever called the police in the '80s or '90s and no one arrived and you wondered why, there's your answer.

Disposing of calls from the public as a way of controlling demand was not employed every day but it was a method that everyone in the control room knew about and used, with some doing it more than others. The local gaffers weren't officially aware of it, like a lot of things we did, but there were some who knew and accepted that it was usually done at times of sheer desperation. It was interesting to observe at very busy times some gaffers would slowly amble out of the control room, coffee in hand, to find somewhere quieter, with few, if any, willing to sit down and pick up a phone. I don't blame them really; the atmosphere was extremely noisy and stressful. On one occasion an inspector calmly wandered from the control room to the property store with his coffee saying, "See you later" and blew his brains out with a shotgun. The corridor downstairs to the rear yard was a terrible mess.

Demand was rising at an alarming rate, and I noted in my diary that calls to Radford Road police station in 1989 totalled 51,634. The following year the end total was almost 20% higher at 59,839. How could this be sustained? There were increasing occasions when no-one was available to attend genuine emergencies. I know the public might find this hard to believe but it's true. It's much worse now. I remember one such occasion I was on the pad when this happened; in sheer exasperation I ran from the control room, picked up a set of vehicle keys and travelled to the job myself. I then returned to the station and sat down in the control room. I only ever did this once but it was a sign that something was clearly wrong.

Working in the control room gave a much greater insight into the personalities of colleagues, learning quickly the difference between the workers and the shirkers. The same hard working colleagues constantly called up for more jobs and regularly visited the control room, in person, asking for work. Other members of the shift would disappear for hours, never to be seen or heard. If they were asked to do a job it seemed they were always busy with other things and unable to help. At the end of the shift they would then wander into the control room and let slip that they'd been bored all day. This is the price of idleness. It began to annoy me that we were all paid the same, regardless of the amount of work we did. This is not unique to the police service of course; everyone at some point has worked with at least one idle bastard.

One of the hazards of indoor work at that time was passive smoking. I'd given up smoking years before and was still jogging in my spare time, so I was aware of other people's smoke without being self-righteous about it.

However, I was working with several heavy smokers and at busy times they would smoke constantly. In only a few hours with two or more smokers in the relatively small room it would often have the appearance of a Moroccan Kasbah. The control room was operated on a twenty-four-hour basis, and so every six months the ceiling was painted white to cover the deepening yellow stain. I began to acquire a cough and frequently experienced headaches and a sore throat. On more than one occasion I contracted pharyngitis, a serious throat infection, and visited my doctor. The first thing he always said to me when he looked at my throat was "Do you smoke?" I occasionally took time off with throat problems, which my doctor and I attributed to passive smoking. The expression was very new, and I remember my inspector, a rather corpulent man who seemed to care little for his own health at the time, told me that I was being stupid, and if I took any more time off in such circumstances I would face disciplinary action. I was told to forget about the whole thing and get on with my work. Undeterred I conducted some research into this new phenomenon of passive smoking.

I contacted the Tobacco Advisory Council, the TAC, which was sponsored by the tobacco industry, and their opponents, the charity Action on Smoking & Health, or ASH. I still have the leaflets they sent me. The TAC's advice came in the form of a very glossy brochure which flatly refuted the existence of so-called 'passive smoking'. Under the title 'Not the real problem' health issues in the workplace were more likely being caused by a phenomenon known as 'sick building syndrome' rather than Environmental Tobacco Smoke, or ETS. The brochure has a picture of two men smiling at one another while seated at a desk; the man nearest the window is smoking, and an extractor fan is seen drawing all the tobacco smoke out the window. A whole page of the booklet then talks about the history of tobacco and how much it formed part of everyday life. Looking at it today the whole thing seems hilarious, but in those days it was meant to be serious.

ASH sent me a simple factsheet about passive smoking, and it was frightening reading. They also sent me instructions on how to apply for a Smoking at Work Policy. Having digested all the facts on 21st December 1989 I submitted a three page General Report requesting Nottinghamshire Constabulary adopt a smoking policy. I still have a copy. It was ignored. A few years later two colleagues in the same control room contracted throat cancer. Only one of them smoked. I'm happy to say the non-smoker is still alive and well.

DRINK DRIVERS

I was becoming more confident in the use of computers so I applied for an Intoximeter course. The Lion Intoximeter 3000 was the large machine in the cell block on which drink drivers were tested after failing the roadside breath test. The machine works by firing a short laser burst through the subject's breath. It can tell by refraction how much alcohol is in the vapour, and is extremely accurate. The small hand-held device used by cops on the street is merely a screening device, and cannot in itself be used as evidence in court.

The Intoximeter machine was regularly checked and calibrated to ensure accuracy, and I found it very interesting. However, not many colleagues agreed, and because it was done on a voluntary basis I became one of only a handful of trained officers. There was no extra money involved, as in most such things at the time, including working in the control room. I'm not saying I was the hardest working cop in the station but idle cops don't volunteer. I undertook these additional roles because they were interesting and they were new challenges.

There should have been at least one or two cops on every shift trained on The Lion, as it was known, but in the following eighteen months I undertook eighty-eight Lion operations. The vast majority resulted in a guilty plea, mainly because of the machine's spotless reputation. However, my Lion operations still resulted in more than twenty court appearances in a relatively short time where I gave evidence against the defendant.

According to my pocket book, on one particular night shift when I started work at 10pm, my first operation was at 11pm, and then I conducted almost one an hour until 6am when I finished work. The majority were brought into Radford Road custody suite by the roving traffic officers from Nottingham's Central Traffic Department in the big 'jam sandwich' police cars, the like of which you rarely see on British roads these days. Don't be fooled by the brightly liveried Highways Agency vehicles that patrol British motorways today. They are not cops, even though they and their vehicles are dressed up to look like the police. They have a power to pull you over 'on safety grounds' but they cannot search or detain you, or issue you with a speeding ticket. They can give you advice but that's about all. I notice drivers slowing down on the motorways when they see these vehicles, and I find it annoying that people are being paid to look like police officers when they aren't. I thought it was illegal to impersonate a police officer?

Usually the first indication that I would be required to perform a Lion operation was when I heard the bell and the rattling of the roller shutter in the basement as the traffic cops drove into the van dock, an area nicknamed 'the bomb bay'. I'd trot down the stairs into the cell block and turn on the machine. The paperwork was a simple standardised form on which you merely filled in the blanks. One of the few professional opinions a police officer can give is whether a person is drunk, and if there's one thing a drunken person is adamant in telling you it is that they are not drunk. The drunker they are, the more they protest that they aren't. Try it next time you are with someone in that condition.

Many people arrested for failing a roadside breath test will therefore be very loud and vociferous in protesting their innocence to anyone in sight. They will then demand their phone call because, according to them and what they've seen on the telly, it's their right. Well, actually, it isn't. The law doesn't allow for anything to delay the process of being placed on the substantive breath testing machine. The argumentative ones were the worst. At every request made of them they would reply with a question and offer verbal, if not always physical, resistance. Apart from denying they were drunk they'd also tell us we should stop hassling innocent motorists and look for the real criminals instead. Everyone who says this sincerely believes cops have never heard it before.

I dealt with a particularly stubborn woman who repeatedly stuck her tongue over the disposable mouthpiece, claiming it was blocked. Several times I removed the mouthpiece and tried another, but on every occasion she claimed a blockage. The mouthpieces were made of transparent plastic so quite what it was supposed to be blocked with, I had no idea. Then she changed her story by saying she didn't have enough breath to satisfy the machine because she'd just had a cold. This same lady had failed a roadside test and so she clearly didn't want the Lion to confirm she was pissed. I spent almost two hours gently coaxing her to give me a sample of breath. She was argumentative and awkward. Her speech was slurred, I could smell wine on her breath and she seemed to have trouble concentrating. In the end I gave up because other customers were waiting.

I had an interesting afternoon in court with her, some months later. The date sadly coincided with the birth of our first child, though I wasn't to know this when she was charged. My wife was admitted to hospital the day before and had been in labour for twenty-four hours prior to the birth at 9am the next morning. The same day at 2pm I was in court, having been awake almost all night. I was very tired and even a little angry at being there in the first place, but the adrenaline of the birth clearly kept me going. I think the anger to some extent came from the fact that certain members of the public very often underestimate the police, and individual police officers like me. I had become quite expert in the use of the Lion, and it was designed to be an extremely simple device. The clear plastic mouthpiece and tube leads straight into the machine with no possible means of obstruction, and yet this drunken idiot continued to claim it was blocked.

The Lion had been designed so that a ten-year-old asthmatic with one lung could provide a sample, or so we were told, though I'm not sure of the provenance of this saying. In any case it was not the force of the breath but the volume, and nothing like the pressure needed to blow up a balloon. I showed the magistrates an example of the disposable mouthpiece which I always carried with me to court, just in case. To counter the argument the defendant brought with her a chest/lung specialist from the local hospital, at great expense to her, in order to inform the court that having recently suffered a bout of influenza, her lung capacity was estimated to be 17% lower than average. But this was not the issue of course. The point of law, and the offence for which she was charged was that she had deliberately failed to provide a sample of breath.

At every opportunity I informed the magistrates that in my professional opinion the woman was drunk. I may have appeared quite confident but such confidence usually comes from knowing what you are talking about. As with any form of public speaking if you have a very good working knowledge of your subject then this will not only help dispel nerves but also make you sound very convincing. After almost an hour in the witness box and some very brief deliberating on the part of the bench she was found guilty. She was banned from driving for twelve months and fined £1000.

I returned to Radford Road and appealed to the duty inspector for the remainder of the shift off work in order to go home to my wife and new baby. I felt very lucky to be granted the rest of the day off on compassionate leave. I was on standby for some short notice leave, which I was then granted. I had the rest of the week off. There was no such thing in those days as paternity leave.

On some occasions the customers for the Lion, as with many other arrests, were extremely drunk. One chap was so intoxicated he had to be supported on both sides by police officers. As he leaned against the charge desk a vile smell began to exude from his person. A dark stain appeared around the seat of his trousers just as some runny little dollops emerged from his trouser legs onto his shoes. The floor area where he was standing gathered excreta in the same manner as a prisoner of war ridding himself of tunnelling material. He was promptly hoisted up and dragged into the toilet where he remained with the door firmly shut until his bowels were well and truly empty. This is one of the few ways to delay the process, if you fancy trying it.

I'd like to know what type of lemonade some people drink too. So often I heard the comment, "I've only had two pints of shandy," just before they blew four times over the legal limit. There's some seriously strong shandy out there. In most cases I remained calm and professional, focussed on obtaining the sample. Better to spend time persuading them at this stage than having another day out at court. I would often spend an hour or more coaxing someone to blow into the machine, in one long, continuous breath until I told them to stop. "Keep going, keep going, keep going," I would say, willing them to do so until the sample was obtained.

The deceitful behaviour presented to me by some of the drink drivers when they insisted they'd only been drinking shandy was insulting. Driving when you are pissed is stupid and very dangerous. There is little wonder the penalties are so high.

THE MIDDLE YEARS

FOOTBALL AND GOOSE FAIR

It's one of life's cruel ironies that when you have a young family you need to work longer hours because of the need to earn extra money. All occupations are the same. My wife quit work for seven years when our children were born, so money was tight, but we agreed to do this rather than spend huge amounts on day care. For the next few years I travelled to work on a moped which only required a few pounds of fuel a week. Riding home at 6am in ten degrees of frost is just bearable, and getting into a warm bed frozen solid was wonderful, if not for the person already there. Travelling to work in heavy rain the water almost always penetrated my clothing so on those occasions I was forced to carry spare socks and underwear. A wet arse was never a good start to a busy shift.

I didn't get many Saturdays off, but in winter I volunteered to work football matches. There were games in the week sometimes too when I was on rest day, and I worked them whenever I could. They were worth about £40 in overtime and we needed every penny. It was known as 'own time football' and we were usually briefed inside the ground along with the match stewards. On almost every occasion I spent the entire match standing on the cinder track around the pitch staring up at the faces of the crowd. We weren't allowed to watch the game but it's not always easy to ignore when thousands of people are following the ball and goals are being scored.

The worst of any trouble seemed to be dealt with by the SOU lads, the Special Operations Unit as they were known. They herded the away fans to and from the railway station in a crocodile system, keeping them isolated from the home supporters. I remember one occasion standing in the sterile area between opposing supporters when it started to rain. There was nowhere to go so I turned up the collar of my greatcoat and carried on. Then I noticed there weren't any clouds in the sky, and wondered where the rain was coming from. The opposing fans were spitting at one another so much it was as thick as rain. When they ran out of spit they threw coins. After the match I collected a small fortune.

On another occasion a man quite high up in the crowd mouthed at me directly 'You're fuckin' dead.' I turned away briefly then looked back at him, and he did it again. I was shocked. What had I done to upset him? I walked to the end of the stand to find a way to speak to this chap. A few minutes later inside the stand the man had disappeared. Maybe I'd imagined it?

On one of the rare occasions I found myself inside the custody area a senior officer was heard shouting for anyone with any knowledge of German. I was about to volunteer when someone presented themselves. There'd been some trouble from the only German person in the world who couldn't speak English. He probably did but was just being awkward. It seemed despite various attempts to extract his name and details no one had managed it. A cop came forward telling everyone "I can speak German," and he confirmed several times to the chief inspector that he could speak the language. Finally, and to a hushed gathering, he said to the German:

"Vot iss your name?"

I understand a little bit of several languages but I would never admit to being able to speak any of them.

Public events such as football matches were very costly to the police, both in time and money. Cops frequently had rest days cancelled which if done in advance meant no extra pay for the inconvenience, and it is still the same today. But a cancelled rest day rightly meant that it was returned to be taken later. The original rest day was probably cancelled because of insufficient staff, but then the same staff whose day was cancelled then took this extra day off, creating another shortage later, and so it goes on. I'm sure successive Home Secretaries would prefer it if police officers never took time off at all.

Every police force has its major events which the public sees as wonderful. For most cops these occasions are quite simply a nightmare. In Nottingham one of the ritual nightmares is the Goose Fair held every year on the first weekend of October. Crime doubles or trebles during the event and gormless people from around the country arrive completely unaware that Hyson Green is one of the worst areas of the city. In the early days of my career it was a huge event for the police. We had enormous mobile catering wagons nearby and cops were drawn in from across the county. Dragging staff from all over never made much sense to me, and they still do it today. People expect you to know your way around and yet they have cops working in areas they've never set foot in before, as though the aim is to deliberately make your staff appear stupid. I've done it myself many times, wandering around for hours or even days with no local knowledge of the area or its villains. From an operational point of view it's only mildly better than being utterly pointless.

Halfway through a shift on Goose Fair duty they'd ram down your throat some awful sloppy meat mixture that I wouldn't feed to my cat today. But if I'm honest, I quite enjoyed it at the time. They were hot meals on cold nights and they were free. Cops are rarely given anything free these days. Policing the fair usually meant terminal boredom, frequently in the rain. I was once told that if you are ever bored as a cop then you are doing it wrong. Okay, try 'fixed point' at the junction of Holland Street and Radford Road for eight hours every night for a week. Standing alone on the same bit of kerb unable to move, save for the yummy slops at half time. On the second night of such unbearable excitement a colleague once brought a hip flask to work which certainly took the edge off the boredom. The public continue to stream by with their kids and balloons and we are told to smile at them. As the night progresses many of the public become quite drunk and so the fun just gets better. In 1990 we started working ten-hour shifts, so what joy that became, standing there for an extra two hours every night.

In the 1980s it was fashionable for some of the locals to cause trouble on the Saturday night of Goose Fair. I remember running down Noel Street towards the fairground with other cops waving my truncheon around over my head and screaming. I think the kids just wanted some fun because as we neared them they disappeared. In later years I spent time in a van, cruising around the fair with other cops. Sometimes we'd turn the windscreen washer jets to the left and squirt unsuspecting members of the public as we drove by. Cleavage and fancy hairdos were prime targets. They'd never guess it was us. Groups of young ladies were obviously the main targets for extra attention, and ladies, if a cop ever tells you, "I'm sure I've come across your face before" it's not meant as a compliment.

On the rare occasions during the fair when I wasn't working fixed point but working normally each shift was spent driving from one job to the next, as usual, taking details of crime. Very often it was from people visiting Nottingham reporting their car broken into. I will never understand why some idiots insist on leaving valuables such as wallets, purses and latterly laptops and other valuables in their cars. You may as well just leave them lying in the street. There are huge problems associated with the theft of a wallet. Credit cards are kept for years by offenders and any form of identity can be used to open store card accounts and all types of fraud. Your credit rating can be damaged for years.

Luckily in those days if a string of offences were thought to have been committed by the same offender, then it was considered to be 'a continuing offence', and only one crime number issued. This was regardless of how many separate victims there were. One morning I dealt with nine cars broken into in a single street in the Aspley area of Nottingham. According to the reporting methods at the time it was one offence. Today the police are supposedly 'victim led' which means each victim gets a crime number of their own. This was one of the reasons why crime rose so dramatically when the more ethical recording methods were introduced.

Statistics could prove anything of course, and they can be manipulated in whatever manner suits. I later saw some of this 'massaging' of the figures which resulted in Nottinghamshire Constabulary along with several other forces getting a very public roasting from the HMIC, Her

Majesty's Inspectorate of Constabulary. The police were caught like naughty schoolboys cheating on their homework, altering the figures in a manner that was euphemistically known as 'unethical crime recording'.

STATISTICS AND STARBURSTS

At times of crisis in any organisation the management often run around like headless chickens, and so it was with our gaffers at Fraggle Rock. Those of us on the ground actually doing the work inevitably suffered. Frequent pointless changes were made in the hope the problem would mysteriously disappear. They changed the people in charge of individual sections, stations and entire areas, and they also tampered with people's shift patterns.

They might change the names of things just for the sake of it in the hope of improvement when all the time no real difference occurs. It probably looked good and someone at Fraggle Rock no doubt gained their promotion from it. This was a constant problem generated by the police promotion system. Sergeant and inspector ranks required the passing of an exam, but above that you needed to get yourself noticed and ingratiate yourself with those higher up. I love the analogy of the police rank structure appearing like a tree full of monkeys. Looking down all you see is faces looking up, but looking up all you see is arseholes.

It seemed that ridiculous ideas were often as valid as the good ones, just so long as they improved your own profile. If your crazy idea didn't work in practice but gained you promotion then it was a success, even if it cost the taxpayer huge amounts to rectify afterwards. To obtain promotion you needed a sponsor, and this still applies today in our wonderful world of equal opportunities. If you don't have some high ranking gaffers looking down on you approvingly, then you've got no chance, or so I'm told. It seems nothing's really changed since the good old days before all the current EO nonsense.

Most of the changes from the small to the enormous were usually dismal failures. Some bizarre decisions were made by management, most of them hopeless, and when you raise your hand to point out the same thing had been tried years before with disastrous results they will say you are a dinosaur, resistant to change. It's not surprising that poor decisions are made by those sitting in an ivory tower insulated from the real world. They say Hitler was not told the truth by his generals until the Red Army was only 400 yards from the bunker.

One of the sadder aspects of policing is that rank seems to be used purely as a means to avoid police work. It is extremely rare to see anyone above the rank of sergeant on the front line actually doing the job, as most senior officers seem to work nine to five office hours. The British Army has a philosophy of leading from the front, and a good leader would never expect their troops to do something they would not be willing to do themselves. Having a much anticipated weekend off with your family cancelled to wander about in the rain all night, knowing those who made the decision remain safe at home with their family can only cause resentment. Occasionally you might see a senior officer with a stick and brown leather gloves wandering about for a few hours appearing very sincere, as incongruous as Simon Cowell queuing for a pea mix in your local chip shop.

In the 1990s crime exploded, and still no-one knew why. It was common to have fifty cars broken into in a single night in the council estates of Aspley and Broxtowe in the west of Nottingham. House burglaries were almost the same. In the Forest Fields area I attended a house that had been broken into seven times. Criminal damage offences were no exception, but the official figures were kept reasonably under control, mainly due to the 'minor damage book'. Anything deemed to be minor in nature, such as a broken window that might cost £10 to fix, was given a minor damage number. This was permissible up to a maximum of £20. The crucial thing about this of course was that it didn't generate a recorded crime number. It therefore didn't exist in the official figures. The public were happy because they were given a vaguely convincing police reference number such as '23/July', and the name of an officer, in case they needed to make an insurance claim. Like many procedures in the police it was something we'd always done but which through necessity grew well beyond its intended purpose. The numbering system started at zero every month, and as the '90s progressed the minor damage book became extremely popular. From a routine amount of around twenty-five a month it grew into hundreds each month, and every police station had a minor damage book, so the disposal of crime in this manner was force wide.

As the crime rate soared the minor damage book began to be used in other imaginative ways. At the scene of a burglary if the offender hadn't gained entry, instead of being recorded as an attempted burglary the crime was given a minor damage number for the broken window or damaged door. The same applied to thefts from motor vehicles, if the car was damaged but nothing had been stolen. Occasionally senior officers would feel obliged to say something about this inappropriate crime recording, and so for a few days we chance of getting away with it. I found it quite surprising everyone wasn't committing crime, the likelihood of being caught was so remote.

More imaginative ways were therefore sought to massage the figures. Changing existing detected non-crime offences into detected crimes was a brilliant method. On more than one occasion I saw a sergeant spend huge amounts of time searching through the hand-written prisoners list, a book where each arrest was recorded. Acting on the instructions of a gaffer each arrest was examined in detail in case it could be changed into a detected crime. A breach of the peace for example was not a crime, but if it was somehow changed to the offence of affray, which is a crime, then it was given a crime number. It was obviously detected because the offender had been in custody. The detection counted at that time, and so even if the prisoner's list book was years old it still counted in the current year. The detection rates soared as a result. Though not illegal as such, it was clearly unethical. Most annoying about this little scam was a person complicit in it later worked in the PSD and approached their role with religious zeal, or so I'm told, showing no mercy to other colleagues caught being similarly unethical. This was hypocrisy of the highest order.

Despite all these efforts Nottinghamshire still had one of the highest crime rates in the country, so you have to ask yourself what the other forces were doing in order to keep their figures down.

At the start of the '90s each working day or night was spent relentlessly driving from one job to the next recording crime. Unless the offender was at the scene waiting to hand himself in to the police the majority of crimes were recorded and forgotten. It seemed we had somehow returned to the policing methods employed during the miners' dispute.

Uniform section had haemorrhaged staff into the new squads and experience was not being replaced. Despite a culture of marking off many crimes as undetected I frequently had twenty-five or more potentially detectable crimes in my docket, with little or no time to deal with them, and every day I picked up more. I should have followed the advice of many other colleagues who simply refused to take on any crime investigations. Some cops never had anything in their dockets. This was due to a combination of being bone idle, and the way they dealt with incidents. They would simply advise the victim there was nothing that could be done. I had a little difficulty with this. I still found crime interesting and if it was easily detectable then why not take on the job and see it through? As a result I began to sink under the pressure of work and needed a break from response duties.

At the end of 1990 I escaped for a while and spent four weeks at training school learning to operate the HOLMES computer system. It was a very intense course but it was good to be away from round-the-clock shifts for a while. HOLMES stands for Home Office Major Enquiry System, and was a database primarily used as the name suggests, in large incidents such as murders. It was incredibly complex and I found the course quite challenging. One of the problems was that once trained in the system you were only ever called in to use it on an ad-hoc basis, and apart from occasional refresher courses it was a while before I used the system for real.

In the late '80s and early '90s the British police began to take riot training a little more seriously. Even today it isn't the various manoeuvres, marching together between the various practice points. Part of our repertoire was the building entry, where a dozen of us using long plastic shields held together as a roof structure would trudge our way up to the door like Roman soldiers, and in turn enter the building. It acquired the nickname 'trudging and wedging' as a result. We were also pelted with real petrol bombs. If the flames came under the shield then you were supposed to drop your chin forward so the helmet visor formed a seal against the chest, but when you did this you couldn't see where you were going. I forgot to do it once and lost most of my moustache. Human hair has a peculiarly strong smell when burnt, even more so when right under your nose.

Day two was spent putting all the theory into practice. Students, police recruits and cops from another division gathered as an angry mob throwing heavy wooden blocks. The instructors would also throw petrol bombs. It wasn't pleasant, particularly on hot days. Then we would be told an entire building was occupied by rioters and we were to go in and remove them. After a successful building entry on the ground floor while being pelted with blocks from above, every room had to be taken individually, with snatch teams running in dragging the 'prisoners' away. In one part of the building we faced the 'mad man in the room' scenario. This involved the biggest member of the training team being completely padded, leaping about wielding a pick-axe handle and shouting "Come on ye bastards!" Three or four cops with long shields would run at the man and press him up against the wall while colleagues rushed in to restrain him. It sounds quite straightforward but it was usually done in complete darkness except for a member of the team flashing a powerful lamp around behind us. It was noisy, chaotic, sweaty and incredibly dirty work. I later formed part of a three-man team who did this for real one afternoon when a drunken neo-Nazi went berserk with a machete and a bottle of bourbon. It actually worked very well, and I was commended for my bravery, but then so were about a hundred other cops standing around at the scene.

During one of the practice sessions I pulled my back, which was not surprising considering what we were doing. It was very painful but I managed to carry on. Some of my older colleagues told me to submit an injury on duty report. I hadn't bothered before, but I was assured that once I had twenty-six and a half years' service I could use it to get a medical pension, as was customary at the time. A lot of cops in their mid-forties were pensioned off early through illness or injury and the final salary pension was immediately index-linked. Such things are extremely rare today. If you're not capable of full duties now you will probably just be sacked.

At the end of the two days' PSU (Police Support Unit) training, as it was called, we felt quite accomplished, but such training was only ever once or twice a year, so we never really achieved a higher standard. It was always practised with different people too, so you couldn't become a close cohesive fighting unit. Again, as with so many extra-curricular activities, it was done on a voluntary basis, with no extra money in it.

Despite escaping from the front line occasionally, whenever I returned my docket was still full of unresolved work. The public don't realise that unless the officer retires or dies, his or her work invariably remains with them forever. Even after lengthy abstractions or annual leave it stays with the same officer. This situation is unchanged to this day.

I was driving around inner city Nottingham from one job to the next, with barely time for a meal break. I didn't mind working hard but for the first time I noticed what was really happening. It had been a particularly busy morning and at midday I requested a meal break. I was turned down several times and informed over the radio: "You're the only one out" so I had to continue. It seemed no-one else was available because they were all busy. I was eventually allowed to return at 2pm when the afternoon shift arrived. I was very tired and hungry. I was shocked when I walked into the station to eat my sandwiches. The canteen was full of cops, both uniform and CID, all sitting around watching England in the World Cup.

HOLMES

In 1992 a Nottingham milkman was bludgeoned to death in his garage. The scene was an incredible mess and at first it was thought he'd been shot in the head. I was told to report to a police station closer to the scene to be a HOLMES indexer for the first time. A conference room on the top floor became the incident room and I started immediately. All rest days were cancelled and it was hard work but financially very rewarding, with four hours paid overtime every day for the first three weeks.

It was very interesting following a murder enquiry from the beginning all the way through to the end. The victim became known as N1, or Nominal Number One. From that moment every other person involved in the enquiry was given a similar consecutive number until eventually there were thousands on the system. I worked with a handful of other cops entering information into the computer, but there were quite a few civilian members of staff involved.

A detective superintendent ran the enquiry, and each task he wanted performing was known as an action. These were in the main hand-written instructions on specific forms, such as 'Seize victim's clothing' or 'Conduct a fingertip search of the scene' and so on. Completed actions were then fed into the computer. Inputting, or indexing as it was known, was mostly straightforward but some witness statements could take hours or even days to index correctly. Each address and name had to be searched for and if it wasn't already on the system it must be created. Every piece of information then had to be linked to another and it was done to some strict rules and conventions, so that all the information was searchable, even the free text fields. Every piece of information was linked to something else; it couldn't simply appear in isolation on the system.

The work was very intense and was made even harder by an obnoxious fat bloke occasionally shouting abuse at people across the office. He'd obviously been to the same charm school as my tutor constable, and the only good thing about him is that he's probably dead now. I don't care who you are, there's no excuse for rudeness.

It was on this enquiry that two detectives spent a whole day looking for a Nottingham company called Unident. They thought it might be connected to the Boots factory in some way, or with the manufacture of dentures. There were dozens of dental practices in Nottingham; perhaps the van belonged to one of them? The action they had been given was to trace a 'Unident van'. They finally returned to the office after an exhausting day to be told that 'Unident' is a HOLMES rules and conventions abbreviation for 'unidentified'.

As the enquiry progressed there were frequent visitors to the incident room asking "Has your wonderful machine found out who the murderer is yet?" in only half-joking comments. A huge piece of paper ten yards long and a yard wide was fixed to a wall and it was the first time I'd ever seen a mouse, not the furry variety, but the type linked to a computer. It was used to construct an enormous Anacapa chart linking everything together. The victim was researched extremely thoroughly. All his friends and family were identified, work colleagues, school friends, girlfriends, everyone he knew dating right back to his birth. They were all investigated on 'TIE' actions, Trace, Interview & Eliminate, and everything about his private life scrutinised for a possible motive. Think about your own life and how many people you may have upset over the years. It was quite revealing.

Eventually it was discovered the victim had been seeing someone else's girlfriend, and when the boyfriend found out he lost his temper. He was pumped up on steroids and smashed the victim's head open with a baseball bat. It was one of the oldest motives in history.

At first the suspects were 'invited' to the police station for interview and not arrested. I thought this was strange, and very different to how the police usually operate. In the early days of my service people were 'banged up' and left to sweat in the cell for hours and then repeatedly interviewed in order to get the cough. The PACE Act changed this of course. There was now a limited amount of time someone could be kept in custody, and the clock started ticking as soon as they were arrested. You'll hear this on some of the more authentic cop dramas when they refer to 'the clock's ticking'. It's easier to get a time extension for serious crime but why do this if the suspect would come in of their own free will?

They were both interviewed under caution, but not under arrest, and then allowed to leave the station. Human beings are flawed creatures. In the next few days the suspects couldn't help boasting to others about how the cops had nothing on them and they'd just got away with murder.

They were both arrested and eventually convicted of killing the milkman. It was interesting to note that old fashioned policing still played a significant role in the offenders' capture. Purely by chance one of them had been name-checked by a routine traffic patrol close to the scene just after the murder, which caused them both to be linked to it right from the start.

In the same year I was given more overtime when I took part in Operation Container. As the crime rate soared British prison's began filling up and Nottingham's Central Police Station took serving prisoners for a while. It was very lucrative and quite interesting. Many of the prisoners were serving long sentences. No doubt they resented the conditions in police cells, they were far from ideal, but a lot of them didn't bother to dress, shave or even wash, but why would you? Some had to be split up too, because they were doing questionable things to one another. I could only guess.

Every year at the height of summer Nottinghamshire Constabulary held their Force Gala at Epperstone Manor. It was a huge event with stalls, games, live music and a few surprises. The mounted section provided wonderful entertainment, and the horses were particularly popular with children. The dog section's display was dramatic, with a padded criminal running across the huge playing field being brought down and partially eaten by one of the Alsatian dogs. There were police cars and motorbikes available for perusal and it was a wonderful event widely advertised in local media and usually well attended. There was always an excellent family atmosphere with a beer tent and static displays, all fantastic for public relations.

I was shocked when I heard years later the force had decided to sell the manor house. Everything was sold, including all the land. It was a sad day, but no doubt driven by increasing financial restraints. The '80s and '90s had seen huge investment in the police service, at a time when crime was rising sharply. I suspect people began wondering where their money was going. You can buy some of the manor now; it's been renovated and turned into luxury apartments.

In addition to hearing about the loss of Epperstone I later found out that cops were no longer being sent to RAF Dishforth. For a time Nottinghamshire recruits were sent to a training establishment at Ryton on Dunsmore, near Coventry, until even that came to an end. New recruits began attending further education colleges, mixing with ordinary students. In my naivety I wondered if they cleared the car park every morning at 6.30am for drill. I was astonished to hear they didn't even learn any drill. No parades, no marching about of any sort. It was all gone, as were residential training courses. No more saluting, standing up for senior officers, pressing of uniforms and bulling boots. Little wonder that nowadays you often hear senior officers addressed by their first names, and cops openly challenging orders over the radio. The old forms of discipline, and to a certain extent pride in the job as a vocation, began to evaporate. It was gradually replaced by a kind of passive-aggressive, retrospective discipline, whereby even the smallest error made years before could now get you into trouble. Nottinghamshire also dropped the rather quaint title of Constabulary and became Nottinghamshire Police.

When working on response duties my arrest rate was high, averaging between seventy and a hundred a year. If this doesn't sound a lot then bear in mind the majority of these cases then required prosecuting. Another fact the public probably don't realise is that the prosecution of offenders is usually done by the arresting officer. When the

CPS, the Crown Prosecution Service, began operating in England in 1986 I thought we were in for some radical changes. I imagined cops would no longer have to prosecute offenders; it would all be done by the CPS. What a brilliant idea it was, freeing up police time in this manner. Sadly it hasn't worked like this. Every bit of evidence still has to be gathered by the arresting officer, all the statements, exhibits, interviews, paperwork, everything connected to the case. The prosecution file for an incident with two or more offenders could take weeks to prepare, and even then it was likely to bounce back from the CPS when they asked for additional statements or exhibits. As a response cop these files still had to be done in-between responding to yet more incidents every day. It was a never ending cycle, like Sisyphus rolling his stone uphill forever. You could never achieve a point where you'd finished everything, and this continual absence of closure can sometimes feel quite draining. Nothing has changed. At least after the introduction of the ten-hour shift system things improved slightly. The biggest difference was that instead of just three days off after a week of night shifts we now had six consecutive rest days. This was wonderful. It meant of course that if you could book your night's week off you'd effectively be given two weeks off work. I had a young family, so this gave me some quality time at home.

Many of the arrests made on response were mundane but some were noteworthy. Good arrests usually occurred because I just happened to be in the right place, which was quite often considering the area and the amount of time I was there. I arrested a young lad for street robbery in the Forest Fields area of Nottingham and it was my first encounter with a person who was already gaining a reputation. He'd just robbed an elderly lady by grabbing her from behind, pulling her to the ground and then stamping on her head. I was driving nearby immediately after the incident. The first thing the lad said to me was, "You can fuck off till I speak to my solicitor!" He kicked, screamed and threatened violence, and was horrible. He was eleven years old.

I remember my interview with this lad. His mother wasn't interested in attending the station, and no-one seemed to know who or where his father was. Consequently I interviewed him with his solicitor, an additional on-call 'appropriate adult', and a social worker. There were four of us seated around this little lad all paid for by the taxpayer, while his legs barely reached the floor he was so small. I spent thirty minutes asking him questions about the offence while we all made notes. It wasn't a difficult task to write down the replies because they merely consisted of either 'no comment' or 'fuck off', or both. I wondered what would become of the lad when he grew up. I noticed his name appeared every now and again on the prisoner's list in-between years of absence. He was one of our most frequent customers, and he still is. The old lady recovered physically after several weeks in hospital, but she never ventured out alone again.

Old ladies were not immune from breaking the law though. I visited a young couple in the Basford area of Nottingham who had been receiving hundreds of nuisance calls over several months. The caller never spoke, but just listened to them asking who it was, pleading and then shouting down the phone to the silent caller. I submitted a request for a trace to British Telecom and drove to the address. We have an image in our minds of such an offender perhaps being a strange, dirty old man, particularly if the calls were mainly answered by a female. The line belonged to a Nottingham address and when I knocked on the door a seventy-three-year-old lady was sitting alone watching *Coronation Street*. The phone was next to her on a table.

She flatly denied making any nuisance calls. I began to doubt myself, she was so convincing. The computer printout from BT was unequivocal; this person was definitely the subscriber. She continued to deny it until I showed her the evidence. After some quiet contemplation she broke down. She'd selected the couple's number entirely at random from the phone book. She'd tried many other numbers but they simply put the phone down. She enjoyed calling the Basford couple because they always spoke to her. She admitted she was terribly lonely.

At Christmas and New Year if not rostered to work we were offered overtime. It meant double time and a rest day in lieu. I took the opportunity to work whenever I could, despite, or more accurately because I had a young family. Our second child arrived in 1993 and for years daddy either came home from work on Christmas morning, staying up for a while until they'd opened their presents or went to work after bedtime Christmas night. If you work shifts then you will know these things are the norm.

In the summer of 1994 a new baby was stolen from Nottingham's Queen's Medical Centre. I spent several weeks working as an indexer on the HOLMES system, assisting the team of detectives to trace Abbie Humphries, who was only three hours old. I could only imagine what the parents must have been going through, and I had real sympathy because of the age of my own family at the time. We had a huge number of calls from the public, which then generated vast quantities of indexing, and Abbie's parents even had a letter of support from Princess Diana. As usual at the start of the enquiry money was no object and we were working long hours on cancelled rest days. The atmosphere in the incident room was tense and there seemed to be a genuine sense of urgency more acute than in the milkman murder.

After a long computer-aided process of elimination Abbie was found safe and well in a house not far from the hospital. She'd been missing for seventeen days. The offender was a young local woman who attended the hospital dressed as a nurse with the specific intent of stealing a baby. Security at maternity units was quickly improved as a direct result of this incident. My diary states I worked 166 hours overtime and claimed £86.84 in travel expenses that year.

THE CRIME DESK

In 1995 crime continued rising at a phenomenal rate and was completely out of control. There seemed no end to its upward progression despite the police being awarded double digit pay rises every year. As a response driver I wondered how much longer this situation could continue, we seemed to be busier every week. I drew a pyramid chart of job satisfaction and workload versus roles within the police, because it seemed to me that a tiny proportion of police employees, mainly the response cops, actually did anything, despite the staff car park being full every day. Nothing's changed; response cops continue to be the hard-pressed front line of policing. It's another strange dichotomy that they have the most daily contact with the public yet within the job their status is lower than that of caretaker. If you stay on response for more than a few years you are seen by everyone else in the job as a fool and by the gaffers as a complete idiot. I asked a colleague who left response for the CID whether she felt sorry for those of us left behind at the sharp end. She simply shrugged her shoulders and said: "No, why should I?" Why indeed.

The amount of crime we were recording was astonishing and it seemed we were on the brink of anarchy. A colleague who retired at this time was so convinced society was collapsing that he bought a croft in the Scottish Highlands in order to escape the oncoming calamity. The tradition of sending a police officer to all reported crime had to stop; there wasn't enough time or staff available. Crime still had to be recorded, and the public hoodwinked into thinking we were doing something about it. How could this deception be achieved? The solution came with the introduction of the crime desk. I saw it evolve from one cop alone in an office with a phone and a kettle, to dozens of cops and civilians sitting in front of computers.

The police service desperately needed an upgrade, as we were still using typewriters in the early '90s. Computer monitors began appearing in offices all around the station, and it seems odd looking back now, but I don't remember any formal training being given in their use, or even any being offered. I think it was just assumed we already knew how to operate Microsoft Windows, which of course many of us did. I remember the first computer we had at home in the late '90s with dial-up internet costing £1,400.

I had a slight head start having been operating the PNC and HOLMES systems, but Windows was entirely new and we learnt from each other. We were told to log in using our six digit pay code and to create a password of our own. Hardly anyone knew their pay code; it was something that was only used for overtime forms, so from then on it had to be memorised.

No-one ever relished using a typewriter, and so when computers arrived in huge numbers the simplest tasks began to take hours. Instead of just two monitors in the control room they were suddenly everywhere, like Daleks at a Doctor Who convention. If you take a look inside a police station today you will see everyone sitting in front of a computer. It's hard to remember the times we didn't have them and we worked for a living instead. It seemed they were here to stay so I applied for as many training courses as I could and soon I had a job on the crime desk.

I was busy at home with a young family and initially the crime desk worked more sociable hours, so it suited me at the time. No allowances were made for sleepless nights spent with sick babies and I needed a break from twenty-four-hour shift work. At its inception there were just two of us and our job was to deflect demand by ringing callers and giving them a crime number over the phone. We were breaking new ground and we were very often asked: "Aren't you coming round to have a look?" or similar. In actual fact there wasn't a lot of point visiting some crimes, but I admit a lot of evidence may have been lost on occasions. If the crime was potentially detectable we were supposed to create an incident and an officer was sent to the address for further enquiries, but we made sure this didn't happen very often. We even asked victims to conduct some enquiries themselves. You might think this sounds ridiculous, but if my car had been broken into on the driveway I would ask my neighbours if they'd seen anything. It sounds simple, but we tried our best to resolve everything ourselves, that was our purpose after all. The work was easy at first and we had time to get our own affairs in order.

In all my service I've probably only fallen out with half a dozen colleagues, but all of them were above me in rank. When I was on response I brought in a man for a meter break when I had been told to work response duties all day. The man needed nicking, and it couldn't wait any longer. The sergeant took me into an office, telling me I'd disobeyed his orders. At first I didn't know what to say to him, because it was true, I had disobeyed his orders, but he began to get personal, and because I wasn't fighting back he threatened me with disciplinary action. This is the way bullies operate. They sense they are having an impact and then apply further pressure and project their own ineptitude onto others. I sat listening to the man ranting at me and eventually I said to him:

"Okay. Try disciplining me for making an arrest and see how far you get," and I walked out the office. Some colleagues were rude when faced with similar confrontations, but it wasn't in my nature. Perhaps I should have simply told him to f-off. Nothing happened about the matter, and the man never tried anything like it again, in fact, he stopped talking to me altogether.

The biggest such problem I ever had was with an inspector, and the sour relationship persisted until I retired. In 1998 a particularly awful family left the street in which I lived. I'd spoken to the family before when one of the adults allowed her twelve-year-old child to drive their Ford Sierra XR4 up and down the street, so they clearly didn't like me. Some of the neighbours put balloons on their houses the day they moved out, the family were so unpopular. My mistake was allowing my wife to do the same. The mother of the child knew I worked at Radford Road and so she drove straight there in person, to complain about my wife's balloons. I thought the size and shape of my wife's balloons were our business and no-one else's, but I was mistaken. A particular gaffer just happened to be on duty at the time. I have no idea what she told him but I passed the office and noticed she was wearing an extremely short skirt. When the woman had left I was then summoned into his office.

"You've been causing problems for a family on your road."

"Pardon?"

"You've been disrespectful and have been abusing your

authority; you've been rude and officious." This was even before I'd said a word. I explained the situation but he clearly wasn't listening. I told him about the time I saw the woman allowing her son to drive and to my astonishment he said:

"You should have rung the police and not got involved. You were abusing your authority."

I couldn't believe what I was hearing.

"What if the child had run someone over and I'd not intervened?"

"You shouldn't get involved," he kept repeating these same words. I was becoming very angry. I should have definitely told him to f-off, but I allowed him to carry on. I still held feelings of deference towards senior officers, and the shiny metal pips on his shoulders were glinting at me, as a reminder of who was talking. But I knew I was right and he was wrong. Eventually, after several minutes, instead of being rude to him I stood up to leave and began walking towards the door. He sprang to his feet and placed himself between me and the door, with his arms extended, blocking my way.

"You're not going anywhere!" he shouted

"Yes I am!" and I opened the door and left. I walked around the building into the night kitchen and sat down. I couldn't believe what had happened. In the next moment the man came into the room.

"You can't talk to me like this, I'm an inspector, and I haven't finished with you!"

I should have approached the matter differently. The man was clearly deluded, and the whole situation now reminds me of a sketch from *Dad's Army*, with Captain Mainwaring desperately trying to assert his authority. At the time it wasn't the least bit funny. A colleague heard the argument and agreed to sit in the man's office with me. Another inspector sat with the man. He and I then spent twenty minutes bickering while my colleague and the other inspector watched on. Nothing ever happened about it and I wasn't disciplined. It was all extremely childish and an example of very poor leadership from a man who seemed to relish bullying.

The upward march of crime continued, and from dealing with half a dozen crimes a day, by 2000 it had become almost intolerable. From the initial two members of staff on the crime desk we then had three. We were located in an office adjacent to the control room and in winter it was bitterly cold and in summer it was baking hot. The first winter we occupied the office we asked for the heating to be repaired. A female civilian administrator came downstairs to feel the cold and a caretaker later fiddled with the convection radiators but still very little heat emerged. We resorted to boiling a kettle dozens of times a day in the hope the resultant clouds of steam would warm the room. In summer we were given an odd machine on wheels the size of a Dalek and told it was an air-conditioning unit. The control room next door had expensive air-conditioning installed which we found out was not for the sake of the staff but because the computers functioned better in a fixed temperature. Our air-conditioning unit was a bizarre machine that required gallons of water every day and a huge flexible pipe to be hung out an open window like a tumble-dryer. The resultant air from this thing was only slightly cooler but saturated with moisture. Everything became warm and clammy as a result and human skin glistened with sweat. I thought I was back in Brisbane at Christmas. The stupid machine was booted around the office for a while until it ended its days in one corner, sad and redundant.

At the time we were using the CRIS system, the Crime Recording Interim System, to record crime. It was a truly awful database and required a small army of civilian clerks to input the officers' hand-written reports. On many occasions huge amounts of money were thrown at it in the form of overtime just to keep it going. Very often it lumbered along weeks or even months behind due to the time lag involved in the inputting, so any searching for missing property or descriptions of suspects was pointless. It was a complete waste of time and yet we were all slaves to it. The tail was very definitely wagging the dog.

One evening in the CID office at Radford Road I was working four hours overtime purely to input crimes into the CRIS monster when a visitor came into the room. There were several experienced detectives also working overtime on the same menial task, which was an astonishing waste of time and money. A man in early middle age sat beside me and enquired as to what I was doing.

"Off the record, tell me what you think of this CRIS system?" he said to me, appearing genuinely interested. I hadn't a clue who he was, and so I decided to be frank.

"It's complete and utter bollocks. It's slow, dated and incredibly time consuming. Look at all this," and I pointed to the huge piles of crime reports yet to be fed into the machine. He frowned, and I demonstrated just how slow the system was at handling data. He looked very serious and frowned the whole time. He didn't stay long.

After he'd gone a colleague passed me saying, "The new chief's in the building, so watch out." It seemed I'd just had a frank exchange with Mike Todd, the new boss of

Nottinghamshire Police. I hope it was nothing I said that night, but a few years later when he was the Chief Constable of Greater Manchester Police he apparently threw himself off a cliff in Snowdonia, poor chap.

The concept of the crime desk obviously appealed to the high command at Fraggle Rock because it was expanded at each station and then centralised. In 2001 I was working in an office with four computers and five telephones. During busy leave times I was on my own and the pressure was unrelenting. Many of us worked very hard on the crime desk but as usual some managed to get away with a fraction of the work. This particularly applied to smokers. By this time Nottinghamshire Police had introduced a smoking policy very much along the lines I had suggested years before. Smoking was permitted in the back yard of the police station, ironically immediately adjacent to the diesel fuel pump. At Radford Road smoking took place in the enclosed yard next to the night kitchen. This meant that in both hot and cold weather smokers would stand with the doors wide open, making a token effort to blow the drifting smoke outside but usually failing. In a small and busy office working with a smoker therefore meant working on your own for ten minutes every half hour; at least an hour a day, seven days a week amounted to a whole day off, standing outside smoking, time that was lost and never recovered. This blatant skiving by smokers is not unique to the police service, but it never seems to be correctly addressed. They would often congregate in huge numbers and it sounded like a party there was so much laughter going on. They were probably laughing at everybody else carrying on with their work, covering for them.

As was customary in those days, poor or non-existent

supervision meant that if you did a good job you submitted a self-congratulatory report called a 'Performance Record' about your achievements. It was around this time that I managed ten years without any sort of written appraisal. They kept paying me, so I wasn't too bothered, but management of staff really was dreadfully poor. It seemed everyone thought we were going to sink without trace, so a deep feeling of malaise spread everywhere, as it has again today.

I interrogated the crime system in the summer of 2001 and I was shocked by the response. Between 1st June 2000 and 1st July 2001 I personally dealt with 2,730 crimes. I had hand-written each of these on four-page crime reports. In a monthly staff newsletter I boasted that I could deal with a customer in less than a minute, from picking up the phone and saying hello, asking them their problem, taking their details and giving them a crime number. I could sometimes bring it right down to forty-five seconds. It was a necessity, as I was writing fifty or more crime reports a day, in-between lengthy phone calls from colleagues, CRIS inputting and filing. I was the busiest cop in the department, at the busiest station, division and police force. It was quite likely therefore that for a few months I may have been the busiest cop in the world!

By this time we were working round-the-clock shifts providing twenty-four-hour cover. I was sure my boast about how quickly I could deal with members of the public would soon result in more staff appearing, but the opposite happened. We were told to give our customers more quality time, not to rush the calls, to ask appropriate questions and to write them on the back of each crime report. This slowed things down considerably, so I produced a small stick-on questionnaire which I created in multiples on sheets of A4 containing all the necessary questions, which I stuck to the back of each report with Prittstick. All I had to do then was tick them as done, instead of writing them out each time. I expanded the questions to include whether Victim Support or Scenes of Crime officers had been requested, and after a while we were all using this system. A few months later I noticed some new printed crime reports arrived. They had been changed on the back to include most of the questions I had used in my stick-on supplement. I later found out a sergeant with a strangely brown nose had claimed the credit for this, as was the custom.

It wasn't the first time I'd been ignored of course, apart from this and my failed smoking policy. On 23rd July 1996 I submitted a report suggesting a Divisional Underspend Quarterly Prize Draw. I noticed Radford Road was underspent by £12,000 that year, and much of it was coal. One of the conditions on which the station had been built was that the heating should be coal-fired; no doubt in support of the miners and apparently the idea of the Labour council. In the boiler room the caretakers therefore had to work like stokers on the *Titanic* to keep the building warm. It had been a good summer so there was money left over. I therefore suggested a monthly cash draw of £1,000 for staff at the station. It would encourage thrift and would be linked to satisfactory work and a good sickness record. I wasn't surprised it was ignored; it wasn't meant to be entirely serious. But the idea of making a connection with sickness is used in every aspect of personnel management today.

On 7th October 1997 I submitted a report requesting the force consider employing civilian investigators, perhaps retired police officers, to assist in crime enquiries. This was primarily aimed at helping response cops manage their time. A solicitor had told me he had a similar workload but had regular use of a clerk to assist him. This suggestion was also ignored, and yet such people are widely used in most police forces today. I once requested a pistol and a machine gun with a thousand rounds of ammunition, but this was also ignored.

On one particularly busy evening while single-handedly trying to operate all the computers and telephones, spinning plates like a demented octopus, I repeatedly had a female caller ring the office from the Aspley area of Nottingham. She was asking specifically for the officer dealing with her case which she wouldn't discuss with anyone else, so I redirected her call. To my disappointment she returned several times like a boomerang smeared with dog shit. After the third or fourth failed attempt to redirect her in exasperation I said:

"Look, I'm sorry, you may as well speak to your dustbin man as speak to me, I can't help you, I'm sorry."

There was a very long pause before she replied: "What did you say?" at which I knew precisely the direction the conversation was heading. "I don't like what you said," she continued, "what's your name?" so I gave her my details and spelt them out to her clearly, before she slammed the phone down. Dealing with the public is on occasions comparable to being a member of the royal family, in that you can't openly fight back in an argument. I suspected this woman was trouble but I was too busy to dwell on the issue. The next afternoon, a sergeant I'd never seen before was waiting for me as I arrived for work. He asked my name but didn't give his own. He insisted we sit in an office while he chastised me for almost an hour about a poor telephone manner. He ranted on about how crap I was and implied I was idle for being on the crime desk in the first place.

"If you desk jockeys can't handle it you should get outside and do some proper police work."

This was just after managing the office almost single-handedly for months and submitting thousands of crime reports. I felt incredibly demoralised by this encounter. I considered throwing him through a window but my anger was checked by a sudden wave of tiredness and apathy. Maybe this had been building for months but suddenly I wanted to give it all up and go home. It suddenly occurred to me that I'd been working incredibly hard for nothing. No-one was bothered, and in fact the fruits of my hard work were to be told I was crap. That night I informed my wife I was leaving the police.

I've coped with being spat at, kicked, punched, thrown to the ground and verbally abused by members of the public on numerous occasions, but in all my service it has been police officers who have caused me the most stress. I seem to have attracted bullies like the school wimp. The incident with the sergeant was the final straw. I'd been suffering from stress on the crime desk for months, trying to run an office on my own when there should have been five people. I started drinking heavily and waking at 4am every morning unable to get back to sleep. I felt very low. I know my wife was concerned so she suggested I visit my doctor.

I was initially signed off work with stress for three weeks, which was eventually extended. While I was off work I saw the world change forever when I watched 9/11 live on the TV. I was contacted by my employers and offered counselling. I agreed, and drove to a beautiful farmhouse in rural Nottinghamshire where I chatted for hours with a lovely lady. What should have been six one-hour sessions eventually became twelve two-hour sessions. We discussed my travelling days and the work on the crime desk and she said:

"Why are you in an office? You shouldn't be inside, it's not you."

It was suggested my employers had been negligent by creating my stress at work, so I saw a solicitor who agreed to take on the case. After a while following several sessions of counselling, as I recovered I lost interest in litigation, so I abandoned the idea.

I learnt to ski, bought a drum kit and a new car. A few weeks later I was back at work. My self-esteem was still very low, and I didn't feel able to discuss why I'd been off sick. We don't talk about mental health issues do we?

TOWARDS THE END

BACK ON THE BEAT

When I returned to work it was to somewhere different, a small police station in the Sherwood area of Nottingham. This wasn't Sherwood Forest where Robin Hood lived, but an inner-city suburb on the main Mansfield Road. It was still wonderful. I retrained on the use of the new rigid speed cuffs, the CS spray, and the Asp collapsible baton. I never used the PR24 side-handled baton, because it came and went while I was on the crime desk. Cops were generally not impressed by it.

There were only four cops working in Sherwood and we had a huge amount of autonomy. The oldest among us was Jim, a lovely, quietly spoken man who was only a few years from retirement. We were an outpost called a 'contact point' situated between the bigger stations of Radford Road and Oxclose Lane. I was able to resume foot patrol duty after many years of driving around in the cars and sitting in the crime desk office, and I loved it. I attended a problem solving course and it seemed I'd be able to return to old fashioned policing. I began to cultivate new teaspots and I became known to the locals. It was all going well until the gaffers cocked it up again.

It was decided to centralise response in the city to one station, and Radford Road was chosen. This meant that instead of each station across Nottingham having their own local response officers, they were all bundled together in the geographic centre of the division. You may think this sounds quite sensible, but it isn't, and it wasn't at the time. Experienced front line cops protested about the idea, mainly because of the logistical nightmare of driving from one end of the city to another, particularly at peak times. A centralised response vehicle could be in the far north of the city and the next moment sent to the far south, and vice-versa, so this was where problems arose. If not in a hurry the traffic was often horrendous, and in emergencies the blue-light runs became much longer with all the extra risk involved. In policing terms the cops were being sent into areas they'd never been before, with no local knowledge and crucially, in my opinion, little regard for the area or its people. If you think you might never see the same people again, then why should you be bothered about them?

It's the same old story when demand outstrips supply, there's an urge to change something, like rearranging the deck chairs on a doomed ship in the hope that it will sink a little slower. My foot patrols came to an end and I was back in a vehicle responding to jobs and dealing with 'handovers': prisoners left by the night shift. Response duties were still very difficult and demanding, so when a job was advertised working in uniform but with a CID burglary team at Radford Road I took it. For the next eighteen months I worked as a Crime Scene Visitor, attending only dwelling burglaries, and it was rewarding work.

Between 1st October 2002 and 1st September 2003 I attended 418 house burglaries. If there was ever any evidence at the scene I'd take witness statements and make the initial enquiries. Very often an offender quickly became known and the detectives on the team would immediately attend and arrest the villains. It worked very well and we managed to reduce the burglary rate significantly. What's the best way to avoid being burgled? Most burglars enter through the back, usually a window, so restrict access to the rear of your house. Keep everything locked, leave a radio on and a light, and make it look as though you have an alarm. If you can, leave a car on the driveway. Make it appear you are at home, though some burglars will carry on regardless, but this is rare. If you have small items of high value you don't wish to be stolen, put them in the loft in a shitty plastic bag. They hardly ever go up there and if they do they would have to search all the other shitty bags you keep up there, so they won't bother. They want cash, jewellery and credit cards, and will plan to be in your house for only a few moments. If it happens while you are in, then you have the right to defend yourself and your family. Any weapon used must be an item you find in haste rather than planned to use. Just don't kill anyone, but if you do, *never* admit that it was deliberate.

Perhaps we should have been less successful because when the figures improved – and in typical police fashion – our team was disbanded.

In the autumn of 2003 I was asked if I'd like to work the north of the city. I didn't know the area but because the job was that of community officer I took it without hesitation. I moved to Oxclose Lane Police Station and began working with some very good officers.

Helen had worked the north of the city for years and was well known. I was incredibly impressed when members of the public would frequently ring her with information that led to important arrests. She would answer the phone and then run out the door shouting a name and we would all follow. I understood the level of mutual trust required for this, and why such policing is priceless. If I could achieve only half this success then I'd become a very good cop. Sadly, and in a similar manner to so many other hard working cops, Helen's efforts were not recognised and she left the department a couple of years later. Richard Branson is often quoted as saying the main reason for his success is the value he places on the people working for him. The police could learn a lot from this, because so often the people they employ seem to be viewed as more of an inconvenience than an asset.

The Bestwood Estate in the north of Nottingham was governed by crime gangs at the time. Colin and David Gunn lived on the estate in converted council houses and ran the drugs trade with apparent impunity. It was decided this should end. Our efforts were hampered by one of our own cops passing secrets to the enemy, but the offender, Pc Charlie Fletcher, was eventually caught and imprisoned, amid a blaze of publicity. I took part in at least one pre-dawn drugs raid in the Bestwood area at that time to find all the occupants at the address sitting around drinking tea, waiting for us.

The CID offices at Radford Road had been bugged as part of the net to catch Fletcher, and a few seasoned detectives were recorded referring to local villains as 'pond life'. These were honest, hard-working colleagues caught up by accident as a by-product of the Fletcher enquiry. The disciplinary action that followed for making these private but candid remarks on police premises was quite frankly bizarre. They were removed from usual duties, told to sit in different rooms and not to talk to one another. Middle-aged professionals treated like five-year-old children. We were henceforth told that any conversation anywhere on police premises *belonged* to the police and there could be no expectation of privacy. No more jokes, piss-taking or gallows humour. You became selective as to who you spoke to, and the content of the conversation. I'm sure the tentacles of political correctness are far reaching, but the police are pioneers.

At one point Nottinghamshire Police were dealing with thirty-six murder enquiries, most of which involved firearms, and the force was struggling to cope. The Chief, Steve Green, admitted as much to the *Sunday Times* and shortly afterwards some extra funding from the Home Office strangely failed to materialise. He made a further comment to the effect that the force found conditions 'challenging' and denied they were unable to cope. The funding then reappeared. He said to me:

"Why should I penalise the people of Nottinghamshire by missing out on some funding, just so I can express an opinion in the media?" If you've ever wondered why serving coppers of all ranks rarely make public comments criticising the government this is the reason. I happened to be in the Chief's office for some advice after I too had a letter published in the same newspaper.

In 2004 we were all issued with police mobile phones. We were encouraged to give the public our numbers and to use them as often as we could. I thought it was a brilliant idea. I didn't have a phone of my own at the time so it was a real help, though we were told not to abuse it. We were even sent an itemised bill every month with advice to pay for any private calls. I don't know anyone who did.

At that time four of us were based in an internal office ten feet across that didn't have any windows. I think it was originally intended as a store room. Most of the time it was very cramped but when the PCSOs, the Police Community Support Officers arrived, it became quite ludicrous.

The arrival of PCSOs in Nottinghamshire Police is probably best described as farcical; at least it was at Oxclose Lane. No-one knew who they were and what they were supposed to do. They appeared one morning, standing around in their bright blue uniforms looking useful but entirely clueless. It wasn't their fault of course, and as individuals they were great people, in fact many of the first intake went on to become very good cops. For weeks they seemed to do nothing in particular, and I can only imagine how demoralised they must have felt as a result. It really was an appalling situation. No-one seemed to be taking the lead on what we should be doing with these people, and I have to say there was a small element of resentment at them being there in the first place. Why employ people to dress like cops when they are not actually cops? I admit to feelings of this sort at first, and to some extent I still do. They are not even a cheap alternative because their starting salary is actually higher than that of cops at £23,000 pa as opposed to £19,000 pa for cops. They couldn't deal with anything or arrest anyone, so what was the point of them?

The PCSOs were assigned to us because their role was seen as similar to ours, that of community engagement, so we were asked to sort them out. They were eventually told to patrol the streets and get to know the community. It was a wide brief, but we didn't know what else to do. After a while their role became better structured within the organisation, but it took some time. Nowadays you'll see PCSOs standing guard at a murder scene, with the media stating 'Plenty of police activity here' and so on, when in actual fact there isn't a police officer in sight. Lots of old ladies used to tell me: "It's nice to see all these police about" when in actual fact I knew they were PCSOs and not cops. It gives an impression there are a lot of cops when there really isn't. In this respect the public are being conned. Many of them do a great job of community engagement, but so often when they find themselves at an incident there's the familiar cry on the radio of: "Can I have a police officer please?" because they can't actually deal with anything, even though they are paid more than many cops. There's nothing worse than being partnered on patrol with a keen PCSO, particularly near the end of a shift, because they are very good at finding things for other people to do.

I understand they have been asked to work beyond midnight to assist police officers, but the majority are in a strong trade union, UNISON, who politely told the police where to go. Many of the more unpleasant tasks such as working unsocial hours are therefore done on a voluntary basis and not by compunction. Meanwhile cops have to do as they are told because they have no industrial rights. The government recently slashed police officers' starting salary by £4,000 pa at a stroke knowing there was nothing they could do about it.

In November I attended my first tenants and residents meeting on the council estate at the local community centre. It was the first time I'd witnessed the depth of passion some people have for the area in which they live. This was the same area many colleagues had told me was 'just full of snaffs' and wasn't worth bothering about. I was introduced to some strong characters, and realised how much effort many people put into helping their own community. One lady had spent forty years volunteering at the community centre, often five times a week, and had never received any financial reward or recognition. I later submitted a report to the Honours Commission and she was rightly awarded an MBE.

Looking around the table at these meetings I decided to make a conscious effort to become as involved in the community as I could. I joined the community centre management committee and realised how precarious the running of such places were, despite their vital role in the community.

One of the first things I noticed at the community centre was how often the roof was being repaired. I saw council workmen scrambling about up there and one of them said he'd been to repair it dozens of times, but local kids just kept ripping it apart. They seemed to enjoy throwing the tiles around like slate Frisbees. I asked why there weren't any spikes at the corners to stop them climbing up and was told it wasn't possible because the kids might hurt themselves. As a consequence the problem had persisted for years. I was sure something could be done so I made enquiries with the council. Within a few months I managed to get some very nasty rolling spikes installed around certain parts of the building, with warning signs. The roof was never damaged again. This is just one example of what's known as Problem Solving Policing. It comes from the personal ownership of a beat, a pride in the area and responsibility. The results can be astonishing.

There were three parts to my beat area: the council estate of around 800 homes, a posh estate of around 500 homes and a large hospital. The middle-class area caused few problems, other than parking issues when staff and patients across the road refused to pay for parking at the hospital. The council estate took up the majority of my time, until whenever there was a crime spree at the hospital.

When I took over the beat area, crime at the hospital was horrendous at between seventy and a hundred incidents every month. I'd been reluctant to get started; it seemed such a daunting task. In 2004 a report was published internally by Nottinghamshire Police entitled 'City Hospital Problem Profile'. Senior officers in the CID were concerned at the amount of crime on the campus. The report fell down through the chain of command like a block of lead until it finally came to rest with me. I don't think anyone knew what to do, so how on earth was I going to tackle such a huge problem?

I decided to introduce myself to the hospital security staff, a group of sub-contracted people working from an office in an old red brick building. I gave them my police phone number and asked them to contact me whenever crimes were reported. I also asked the police control room to do the same. If I was on duty and I was able, then I'd attend the crimes myself, so that I could closely monitor the situation. It was hard work at first because I didn't know anyone on site and I didn't know my way around.

My first customer was a local drug addict who'd been stealing from the hospital for years. I was astonished to find that everyone seemed to know his name and already suspected him of committing a huge amount of crime on the campus. I asked security to ring me every time he appeared. It wasn't long before a computer had been reported stolen and this man had been seen on CCTV wandering the corridors at the same time as the theft. He was seen empty-handed and then a few moments later carrying a bulky item in a bag. He'd done this type of thing many times before and it seemed nothing could be done about it. Clearly this was not the case. I took statements and preserved the CCTV evidence. Soon afterwards I traced the man's address and obtained a search warrant. In his disgusting first floor flat we found a hospital computer stuffed in a wardrobe. He claimed in interview that he'd just found it and was intent on handing it in to the police.

I arrested this man half a dozen times for stealing from the hospital, and each time he was found guilty at court but evaded prison. At that time he had 126 previous convictions. Eventually we managed to get him evicted and moved away because he was caught illegally subletting his council flat.

I went on to arrest a dozen members of staff at the hospital, including two doctors, one of which was masturbating at colleagues in his coffee breaks. I won't go into too much detail here as I've already written another book about it, but it proved to be one of the most rewarding times of my service. I was making a real difference both at the hospital and on the council estate. Rewards come from job satisfaction, and I was getting huge amounts.

RAGE AGAINST THE MACHINE

In 2005 I dealt with a man on the estate for threatening behaviour, the witness statement for which is still used in some training circles today. His eight-year-old son had smashed an old lady's window and I'd taken the lad to the victim's house to apologise. He was under the age of criminal responsibility, so the matter wouldn't go any further. I was then returning the lad in the police van to his home address in order to inform his mother. His father appeared from a vehicle parked outside the address and began shouting at me. The reason the statement was so remarkable was that I wrote it using colloquialisms, in the manner of Thomas Hardy and in the precise language the offender used. Cops always try to use some direct speech when required, in order to add realism, but never quite to this extent. The following is a verbatim excerpt, but I have changed the name:

> *'I stopped the police van and a group of youths began congregating around the vehicle. Jimmy Smith emerged from his vehicle and immediately threatened violence towards me, using such language as:*
>
> *"Come on ye fuckin' bastard, come on ye cunt" and similar profanities. He said, "What ye been doin' wi' me lad ye fuckin' bastard get out 'ere an' al fuckin' sort ye aaht ye bastard."*

I informed Mr Smith that his son had admitted breaking a window and he replied in profanities:

"That's cos you fuckin' med 'im seh that ye cunt he's only eight."

I tried to communicate with Mr Smith numerous times and explain my actions but he seemed in a blind rage and would not listen to me. I noticed he smelt strongly of intoxicants. He then took up a fighting stance at the door of my police van and held both fists up in the air threateningly and repeated, shouting loudly:

"Ger aaht 'ere an' 'al fuckin' 'av ye, ye fuckin' bastard."

There were children and members of the public around the vehicle and I considered alighting from the van and using my CS spray on Mr Smith but after a very quick risk assessment of the situation I thought it may have been unsafe to do so with so many children around. I said to Smith:

"You are not listening to me so I am going."

I reversed down the narrow cul-de-sac and as I did so I heard Smith shouting in my direction:

"Yeah fuck off ye bastard fuck off," and other similar profane language.

I would describe Mr Smith as a white male, rather dirty and shabby looking, with very bad teeth, shaved head with some evidence of scarring on the same, earrings, and some tattoos visible. He was about 5'9" tall and appeared very thin as if undernourished. Apart from using profanities constantly his speech was very rough as if he had been poorly educated, if at all.'

I could have hit the panic button and called for assistance. It was the middle of the day, so there would have been plenty of help around. But I'd encountered the man before, and I knew his history. As aggressive as he was I didn't feel particularly threatened because the windows were down on the van and the doors were not locked, but he made no attempt to assault me. I also knew that what I could do to him after the event would hurt him more than a roll around in the gutter and an empty CS canister. He had relationships with three women across Nottingham, had children with each, and he'd just been visiting one of them.

I wrote this witness statement immediately after the event and took it to the Housing Patch Manager at the nearby housing office. A few weeks later I was present in the County Court applying for an ASBO against him. I watched the judge's face when he was handed this statement and began to read. He raised his eyebrows when he reached the above section and put the statement down in front of him. He removed his half-moon glasses and looked across the court at me and my patch manager.

"I'm satisfied with this, so I'm going to grant an immediate two year anti-social behaviour order on this individual." I was very pleasantly surprised. Even though the evidential threshold is lower in civil proceedings such as this, it was a great result considering I didn't have any other evidence.

Mr Smith never breached the ASBO. His son later became a regular at my music club and I grew to know him very well. I even met his father again several times before he was imprisoned for a serious assault. One weekend a few years later, when on prison leave, Mr Smith hanged himself in nearby woods.

In the same year a community police officer colleague, Darren, set up a youth club for the kids on his beat area. He had soft drinks, a huge TV and a games console. Funding was obtained from various charitable sources and it worked very well. Inspired by Darren's success in 2006 I set up a youth club of my own, based not on computer games, but music. I formed a music club with grant money from a Nottinghamshire charity and rented the community centre two evenings a week. In the early stages both my teenage sons helped, attending the centre for two hours twice a week.

As with any such project, initial attendance was poor. I put ads in the local newspaper and posters in shops and public notice boards. I worked normal shifts and then stayed at work or returned to the community centre in the evening after work. It was entirely voluntary and I was not paid. After a few weeks the kids discovered it and music club nights became very popular with thirty or forty kids running around knocking hell out of the drums kits and electric guitars. It was an astonishing success and even I was surprised.

After a while some of the older kids became more serious and found it difficult to progress with the young ones constantly distracting them. I decided to run Tuesday nights for young pre-teens and Thursday nights for teenagers. A small group of teenagers attended every Thursday and were so keen that I often found them waiting at the door when I arrived. Because I was on the community centre committee I had my own keys and store room for equipment. I could only play the drums, so my sons taught guitar and keyboards. I also arranged and paid for a few of the keener members to have professional tuition in Nottingham. I bought a PA system and the lads learned by ear how to play songs by Muse, Metallica, Led Zeppelin and Rage Against the Machine.

After a year all the effort paid off when the teenagers became quite accomplished rock musicians. The group called themselves *Convicted,* though few of them actually had any convictions. I was thrilled when lads from some of the roughest families on the estate became involved in the music club, and who in turn invited their friends along. I was working with some of the local target criminal burglars and thieves and we were on first name terms. There were echoes of the relationship my first sergeant had with the villains he drank with in the Smiths Arms many years before. The trust I gained took some time to build, and with some it was hard work, but I knew it was worthwhile. Sometimes when walking the estate in my uniform I'd be approached by a group of lads who would say, "You're our music teacher, why are you dressed like that?" Eventually I knew almost every young person on the estate, and the majority of the troublemakers were members of my music club.

It's a very difficult balancing act between the informal instructional role of music teacher, and operational uniformed cop. It was a steep learning curve for me, and I did make many mistakes. In the early stages there weren't enough adults present, and I struggled to cope with the sheer numbers in attendance, but my sons were a real help. For the first time I realised how satisfying teaching can be. Of course there were many occasions when I wondered why I was doing it, but then there would be times when everything worked well and I realised that as the facilitator, none of it would have happened without my efforts. Such rewards are worth more than money.

Some of the kids were 'challenging' as the modern saying goes. To be frank, quite a lot were noisy and bloody awkward. I only had one major problem on a music club night and it only lasted twenty minutes. An unknown youth from a different estate had been disruptive all night and at the end refused to leave. As I took hold of him to escort him to the door he tried to head-butt me. I brought him to the ground and handcuffed him. I always kept my flexible cuffs in my jeans pocket. He had been unaware I was a police officer, so when I told him the shock on his face was priceless. After a tearful apology I let him go. I suspected a complaint might be forthcoming and it did, a few weeks later. It wasn't from the lad or his mother; they thought I'd acted appropriately, considering he later confirmed that he was indeed intent on head-butting me. The complaint came from a youth worker.

My inspector summoned me to his office and in essence told me the police could no longer lay hands on anyone unless it was to make an arrest. I was shocked by this news. We were not allowed any physical contact whatsoever. I decided to circumvent this by arresting everyone I touched, or at least whenever I needed to I'd utter the words "You are under arrest", and then de-arrest them moments later, which was apparently acceptable. It sounds absurd but this was the result, and it was all about being risk-averse and covering your back.

From an operational point of view the music club was brilliant. I knew who my targets were, where they lived, who they associated with and even the clothes they wore. If reports came in of anti-social behaviour in the vicinity I could tell even from scant descriptions who the perpetrators were likely to be. I'd visit mum and speak to her, and the problem was usually resolved without the need for any formal action. Many of the parents knew who I was and what I was trying to achieve with the music club. I was keeping the kids active, giving them something to do, teaching them a life skill and steering them away from trouble. I handed out guitars and drum kits across the estate, with a promise from them that they would be used for practicing. I rarely lost any equipment, and for every drum kit in the estate there would be half a dozen or more kids using it.

I destroyed barriers between the youth of the estate and the police, which was incredibly important. It was an area officially designated as having some of the worst rates of social depravation in England according to the government's own statistics, and so any help was appreciated. The most depressing aspect of life on the estate was that the kids had very low expectations. They didn't think they'd ever achieve anything and seemed mired in hopelessness. I saw it as my job to break this link as much as I could. I was always disappointed therefore when I heard some of the kids tell me of response cops driving by telling them to fuck off.

Convicted played their first public gig at a neighbouring community centre just before Christmas 2007. They opened with a young lad playing *Smoke on the Water* very badly, but I could see he was chuffed with it. This particular lad had some serious behavioural problems which tragically led to him taking his own life a few years later when he was only fourteen.

The following summer the older regulars of the band played in Nottingham city centre, at a council event in the Old Market Square. They opened with a blisteringly loud version of *Wake Up* by Rage Against the Machine, with the lead singer making full use of the radio mike, wandering around in front of the temporary stage. Then without stopping they played *Killing in the Name of* followed by

Metallica's *Enter Sandman, Sad but True*, and the Muse songs *Plug In Baby* and *Time is Running Out.* They sounded brilliant and the volume was cranked up beyond eleven on the music club's three hundred watt Marshall amplifiers. I'm not sure passing shoppers knew what was going on! You can see for yourself because some of the music club sessions including this gig are still on YouTube, if you search for Edwards Lane Music Club.

I suppose it might seem odd, a serving police officer helping to create this scenario. It seemed even weirder when you take into account our gig bus was a fully liveried police prison van, used to scoop up drunks on a Saturday night. It was ideal transport, mainly because I could park it anywhere, and the kids loved it. The next summer and for the following two years they played the Sherwood Festival on Woodthorpe Park and a gig in Bulwell market place, on a lorry stage. Convicted also played a set at the Nottingham Playhouse, but the gig didn't go very well. It's strange how some gigs just don't happen the way you want them to! If you've ever played live you'll probably know what I mean. Because the prison van went everywhere with us, we never encountered any trouble.

Between gigs and the music club meetings I rewarded the regular attendees with trips away. I took some to the local Rock City music venue, and to see Metallica at the Nottingham Arena. I rented a council minibus and took five kids to see Muse at the Hallam FM Arena in Sheffield, and Kasabian at the Nottingham Arena. The best concert, however, was in June 2008 when I took three lads to Wembley to see Foo Fighters, in my own car. Anyone with any knowledge of this gig will know it was the night Jimmy Page and John Paul Jones came on stage and played some

Led Zeppelin songs. All my hard work with the music club was rewarded in a single evening!

I'm not conceited enough to claim all the credit but at both the hospital and the council estate crime rates began falling rapidly. It was my aim to create a village atmosphere on both the council estate and the hospital campus, where I was known by as many people as possible. The idea was that if you thought you were known by the local sheriff then you may be more reluctant to cause trouble. It works well but creating it can be very time consuming, and you can't afford to let up even for a few weeks.

By 2006 crime was falling anyway, as mysteriously as it had climbed in the '80s and '90s. No-one knows the reasons for this fall in crime which spread across the Western world, though there have been many theories about it. I personally think it may be connected to lead-free petrol and better computer graphics. Science fiction writer William Harrison predicted in 1966 that the masses would one day be pacified by huge viewing screens in their homes and wouldn't often venture outside at night.

Other beat areas were continually plagued by anti-social behaviour. In 2009 there was very little on my estate. Kids are great at doing what they do to amuse themselves in a way that often annoys others, messing about and causing a general nuisance. Today this is called anti-social behaviour. You and I did it when we were kids too, but in those days it was just called 'playing out'.

I developed a good working relationship with most of the city council youth workers and they began to help a lot more. This was formalised with a joint working partnership agreement, and the youth club eventually became a regular event managed by youth services, with my music club added on. One of the criteria they insisted upon was that I should be CRB checked, Criminal Record Bureau checked, for working with kids. I agreed, and they paid for it, but it struck me as a little absurd. I couldn't become a cop if I had a record, and if I acquired one I would have been sacked almost immediately.

Every time I ran out of money I searched locally for more grants. The application forms were a regular hurdle and each time I had to show accurate accounts of where the money had been going. I kept all my receipts and luckily my books were regularly audited by some brilliant community accountants who worked for free. Towards the end I was astonished when I realised I'd spent over £27,000 on the council estate kids.

My efforts were recognised in 2007 when I was awarded the title of Community Police Officer of the Year. I'm not sure I did anything more than anyone else, but my sergeant at the time was good at submitting flattering reports about his staff, and I was grateful. Darren, my colleague with the computer game club, had won the same award, and another colleague, Gary, ran a fishing project for kids on his beat, which was equally successful.

It was nice to be recognised, and my wife and I travelled to London with the assistant chief constable for the national finals. The event was exciting and the food was lovely, but a lad from West Yorkshire police won the national prize. I also attended Lancaster House in London where I met the Prime Minister, Tony Blair, along with hundreds of others from all three emergency services. It was apparently his way of saying thank you to us all, which was nice.

While very busy with the music club two evenings a week, my work at the hospital was as demanding as it was rewarding. I was locking up a lot of people, some visiting criminals and thieving patients. I was juggling my time between the two housing estates and the hospital, and I was never bored.

SURVEYS AND INDISCRETIONS

In the summer of 2006 I was sent with other community police officers on a management training course run by Derby College. It was called 'Introductory Certificate in First Line Management'. We were expected to manage the rapidly increasing number of PCSOs on our beat areas and so this was intended to be of some assistance.

We were tasked to research and present a project entitled 'Suggestions for Change', and it could be anything connected to improving our employer's working practices. One colleague chose improving the uniforms, another the use of vehicles, and for a while I hadn't a clue what to do. Eventually I decided to make a suggestion around a 'clocking on' system for police officers, purely because so many colleagues seemed to be doing precisely what they wanted and were, quite frankly, taking the piss.

As a member of the public you might be surprised to hear this, but cops do not have a clocking on system when they arrive for work. You probably think it wouldn't be necessary; cops are honest people, surely? Cops are human beings too, so if the sun shines, if they are hung over, or if their kids are late for school, then just like everyone else they might be late for work, or not turn up at all. In the early years of my service when the organisation was tightly run and discipline was stricter, there wasn't a problem. But latterly, with less discipline, a culture developed where almost anything could happen, and it very often did.

I devised a three-page, ten question 'Supervisor's Questionnaire' and issued a copy to thirteen sergeants in various departments across the city division. The results were not particularly scientific, but nevertheless they were astonishing and even I was surprised:

1. Six out of thirteen supervisors (46%) stated at least one or two members of their staff were late for work or left early in an average day.
2. Eight out of thirteen supervisors (61%) stated one or two members of their staff were late for work or left early in an average week. Two of these supervisors actually stated that three or more staff were doing this in an average week.
3. Three of thirteen supervisors (23%) stated they suspected they had some staff on their team who were not working the minimum hours.
4. Eight out of thirteen supervisors (61%) stated they had been unable to contact a member of staff at least once or twice in the last six months.
5. Four out of thirteen supervisors (30%) stated they had to speak to the same person more than once regarding their time-keeping.
6. Three out of thirteen supervisors (23%) stated they had used, considered, or threatened the use of the discipline procedures against a member of staff regarding their time-keeping.
7. Seven out of thirteen supervisors (53%) stated supervision would be easier if the organisation were to introduce a formal clocking on and clocking off system.

8. Seven out of thirteen supervisors (53%) stated the organisation would function better generally if such a system were introduced for all staff.

The majority of these absences were unauthorised. Cops were therefore stealing time from their employer on a wholesale basis. It demonstrated an appalling lack of will and discipline amongst the majority of the supervisors. Could this be the unintended result of sending new recruits to an ordinary FE college? It seemed that many hard working, conscientious cops were going unnoticed and unrewarded while some of their colleagues blatantly took the piss.

My solution to the problem was the use of the police identity card, the Warrant Card, as it was known, to be used at a machine inside the building. The cards were already linked to the main entrances on the swipe system, so the IT department could presumably arrange this without too much difficulty. I drew up a nine-month schedule of change associated with the introduction of the system with progress and monitoring by various departments until it had been successfully rolled out across the force. There were 2,499 cops in Nottinghamshire at that time. Even if a quarter of this number was frequently late or absent in an unauthorised manner then a huge amount of time and money was being lost. More annoying to me was the obvious fact that those of us who were conscientious had to work that bit harder.

I submitted my report; a copy of which I know went to certain senior officers. I also kept a copy for myself. I passed the course and was awarded my certificate. I expected some interest in this work, but my suggestions for change disappeared, along with the report. The courses also came to an abrupt halt. I suspect some senior officers didn't wish for a clocking on system either. Could it have been because some of them were the worst offenders?

They've since tried to address the issue by making everyone book on duty with their own personal issue *Airwave* radio. But many cops circumvent this by not turning their radio on all day, and so it continues.

I am always curious to see other points of view on a range of issues, so in 2006 and 2007 I attended as many training courses as I could. I spent a day on a 'Gay Awareness' course, another on a 'Gypsy Awareness' course, a 'Migrant Workers Awareness' course, an 'Autism Awareness' course, and an 'Islam Awareness' course. All were very interesting.

The Gay Awareness course was conducted by an overweight, middle-aged, ex-Metropolitan police detective with a beer belly and a pock-marked face. I could tell he had a huge amount of life experience in the police and he told us of many gruesome incidents and hardened criminals he had dealt with in London. He was irreverent and refreshingly frank, and reminded me in every way of Philip Glenister's colourful character Gene Hunt in the TV cop series *Life on Mars*. He seemed very masculine and I found myself occasionally glancing at the door for the gay instructor to waltz in all dressed in pink and speaking like Larry Grayson. This didn't happen because the hardened detective from London was the gay instructor. That was the whole point of course. He told us about his life at work in the '70s when he made up the names of various elusive girlfriends he'd been shagging all weekend, in order to fit in with his work colleagues' banter. All the time he had a male partner he could never discuss because he knew he'd be ostracised as a 'puff', a 'bender' or a 'queer'. It was very sad to hear, but then in later years when he finally came out he described how it was as though he'd been released from a life sentence in his own personal prison. It was a brilliant day's input and utterly shattered all gay stereotypes.

I was equally astonished by the Islam Awareness course, but for different reasons. A dozen of us were seated in a large happy-clappy semi-circle in the classroom, as is the modern method, waiting for the instructor to arrive. A man walked into the room dressed in long white robes and wearing a hat that looked like a white fez. He stated he was a serving cop, though I'd never seen him in uniform or driving a police car on the front line. He stated he was of Pakistani origin but was born in the UK. He told us some brief details of the Quran, the Pillars of Wisdom and so on. I'd read of TE Lawrence's exploits in Arabia, and of course I'd lived in the Middle East for eighteen months, so it was very interesting. Then he asked if anyone had any questions.

A colleague spoke up:

"What do you think about the use of alcohol in this country, as you said in Islam it is forbidden?"

Without any hesitation the man replied: "We will never be reconciled to the way you drink alcohol, *never.* We will *never* accept the way your women dress either, and get drunk the way they do. We will *never* accept your way of life. We will *never* accept this as true Muslims."

He spoke with a great deal of self-assurance bordering on arrogance, and with a deliberate emphasis on the word 'never'. The room was stunned into silence. No-one dared ask another question. I found it curious that he used the words 'your' women and 'your' way of life, when he'd already said he was born in the UK. I immediately pondered the thought: *What hope was there for integration?*

This experience had been on my mind so much that a few weeks later I sent the following email to the training school:

'I am surprised to see Notts Police is still sending people on the above course. I myself have attended such a day and found it interesting as I realised how rigid, intractable and intolerant the Muslim faith is, and it went some way to reinforcing my own stereotypes of Islam. To that end it was an interesting day. However, now that the government has officially discredited 'multiculturalism' and deemed it to be a failure, I would have thought such a course would now cease?'

I was aiming to provoke a reaction, but I heard nothing for several weeks. The course needed to change as it was clearly having the opposite intended effect. Typically in Britain's modern police service, when something even remotely controversial is said in this manner a straight answer or a debate about the issue just doesn't happen. All you get is a bollocking.

I received this email from a gaffer:

'Can you come and see me on Monday, say 11am, to discuss an email you sent to training following your Muslim Course.

Thank you.'

I knew the chap reasonably well and I didn't have a particularly high opinion of him. I remember in the '80s, when we were both constables, being sent with other officers to a serious assault on Radford Road outside the Smiths Arms. The offender had dropped a bunch of keys in the street which were crucial to the investigation. It was 9.30pm and we were off duty at 10pm. Walking together we both saw a bunch of keys in the road. He looked at me and said: "I haven't seen 'em!" and walked away. He went home at 10pm while I remained behind to book the keys into the property store and provide a witness statement. I was late off by over an hour. Though he was on a different section on another occasion, we were both sitting in a response car near the police station when as the driver he was called to attend a domestic incident in the Aspley area of Nottingham. He had his feet up and wasn't doing anything. To my astonishment he said over the radio: "I'm busy taking a statement at the moment, is there anyone else can attend that?" as he turned to me and smiled like an accomplished liar. Someone else was then sent to the job. He frequently took two hours or more for meal breaks, he never seemed busy and the word 'conscientious' was clearly not in his vocabulary.

I explained what had happened on the Islam course and exactly what had been said. Almost immediately he dismissed my opinions, telling me I was wrong to send the email and the content was also incorrect. It was not up for debate. He then said to me:

"It's not for Muslims to change their way of life it's for us to adapt to theirs. We have to be sensitive as to where we drink alcohol and how we dress." I couldn't believe what I was hearing.

"What? Are you serious?"

"Yes I am. In fact you are lucky I'm not taking this matter down the discipline route. Don't send any such emails like that again."

I was astonished. What was happening to race relations in Britain? The London bombings of 7/7/2005 had surely demonstrated there were real problems in Britain with a failure to integrate.

This gaffer reminded me the police and other public bodies in Britain were now under a legal obligation to promote diversity. When did this happen? I don't remember signing up to become a political evangelist. The job was hard enough without having to actively promote a hare-brained government idea. I thought the police were supposed to be independent of politics anyway? It seemed we were being as cynically manipulated as during the 1984 miners' dispute, but in a much more subtle and pervasive manner. What if the government suddenly decreed the police should actively promote Richard Dawkins' *Flying Spaghetti Monster*?

The Home Office finally became concerned about radicalisation of British born Muslims by creating the 'Prevent Strategy', which was supposedly designed to put a stop to it. Years later some places on the Nottinghamshire Prevent Team became available and so I applied. I considered myself fit for the role having lived in the Middle East, with some knowledge of Arabic and Hebrew. I studied the Prevent policy document and as I turned the pages I wondered when the really useful strategies would start, but they didn't. It was 90% waffle and politically correct tip-toeing. I thought then how the whole thing was doomed to failure, but at least working on the team might be interesting, and remove me from shift work for a while.

I turned up at the interview early and primed, my head full of job-speak nonsense you need to pass interviews these days. I introduced myself and was asked to sit and wait for a while before my interview. All seemed to be going well until the waiting continued for half an hour, and well beyond the time of my interview. What was the delay? I was then told by a person in plain clothes that I was no longer suitable to apply for the post. I asked why.

"Oh, well, it's connected to some comments you made about Islam a few years ago. We can't have you on the team because of it, sorry." That was it. No recourse to appeal. Clearly someone had made a phone call. My 'unofficial' file had been consulted and the email discovered from *four years* before. It seemed I would continue pounding the corridors of the hospital.

The appeasement of Islam in 2006 was typical of the dangerous politically correct nonsense in existence at the time. The situation grew progressively worse and in the last few years Islam has been deliberately singled out by many authorities in Britain for preferential treatment. 'Equality under the law' is the saying, but clearly some are more equal than others. I don't care who you are, no-one should be favoured by a country's law enforcement officers.

I suspect the main reason for this is simply fear of upsetting Muslims, and fear of being accused of racism. It's not the first time the police, and no doubt other public bodies, have been lenient in their dealings with a minority. I was even guilty of it myself at times. An accusation of racism can result in immediate dismissal from any job in the public sector today, and even imprisonment. In the latter half of my service I became reluctant to stop a motorist if the driver was from a visible minority, particularly if I was on my own. "You've only stopped me because..." was a common comment. The job was hard enough, so why would you want to create extra problems and scrutiny from the PSD? I'd heard a rumour that someone high up in the IPCC, the Independent Police Complaints Commission, had been heard saying about police complaints "There's no smoke without fire", which is outrageous if true. It would mean there is now a clear presumption of guilt on the part of police officers.

The same thing happened in the '80s after the police were repeatedly given a bloody nose by vociferous members of the West Indian community. As with the miners' dispute I could see both sides. Genuine grievances and feelings of being disenfranchised have an obvious cause and effect. Some of the greatest changes in society occurred as a result of civil unrest, but not without a great deal of suffering.

Militant Islam is a fearful entity, and so almost anything is sacrificed in order to keep it securely in the box. It is easier for everyone to let something go rather than pursue it and cause trouble. The ultimate manifestation of this attitude is of course what's happened in Rochdale, Rotherham, Luton, Derby, and other British cities where Pakistani men have been apparently deliberately permitted to abuse young girls. The unintended legacy of such leniency has now caused increased fear and distrust of Muslims, thereby causing further community tension.

But the problem continues to worsen. Every year British police are given particular lengthy instructions regarding Ramadan, and how they should be careful when dealing with Muslims. The tone, if not the actual words, mean that cops should avoid them for a month every year. No other group in society is in receipt of such blatant favouritism. We were told not to eat in front of Muslim colleagues during Ramadan fasting, in case it upset them. There were around forty people in the last department I worked in and a single Muslim who wasn't the least bit religious and didn't care at all, but still we were given these orders. Why?

In 2005 Trevor Philips, the chair of the Commission for Racial Equality warned of increased segregation between ethnic groups in Britain, and David Cameron admitted in 2011 that 'multiculturalism' in Britain had failed, and as a concept it was now dead. Ask yourself this question, how much do you known about Sikhism, Judaism, or Islam?

How many friends and acquaintances do you have from other communities or faiths? If you live in middle-class suburbia I would guess it's close to nil. A Sikh colleague once showed me some photos of a family wedding and explained the food, the dress and the rituals that took place. I asked her how long she'd lived in Britain, and she replied, "I was born in Derby." I knew nothing about her way of life. This shouldn't happen.

People have a tendency to fear things they don't understand. There are areas of Britain that no longer resemble this country. Minorities have been allowed to ghettoise themselves and have failed to integrate. This is a disaster for Britain. My suggestion for a solution to these British ghettos is a radical one, but it's been done before. Every city in the country has undergone re-housing of huge numbers of people during the slum clearances. We have poverty in concentrated areas now, but it's not financial. These areas need to be cleared and the people moved, welcomed and integrated into the rest of society, now, before it's too late.

We are all equal under the law, and preferential treatment should not be given to anyone, whoever they are. Neglect of duty should be feared more than upsetting any potentially vociferous minority. The current Home Secretary stated recently that 'institutionalised political correctness' was to blame for the Rotherham child abuse scandal. Only a few years ago the police were described as 'institutionally racist'. You can't have both, so make up your mind what you want, but do it quickly.

The government created this mess; it's their job to sort it out.

CANNABIS AND CACK

I attended more training courses. We regularly had first aid courses, which were mandatory and one of the few useful things I ever learnt in the police service, apart from being able to tolerate idiots. I also attended a Final Warning Clinic course. Restorative Justice was supposedly a new concept. The offender, usually a young person, was forced to confront their offending behaviour, sometimes with the victim. It had been trialled and was deemed to be a success. Usually it meant the offender was given a final warning, and next time he or she would attend court. This wasn't a new concept of course. I'd been doing it unofficially for years, as many of us had. It's called good coppering. This formalised the process and was interesting, even though there was so much mind-boggling waffle as to make it almost incomprehensible. We were supposed to read pages of formal jargon to the child and their parent/guardian/older sibling or whoever could be bothered to turn up with them, but most of it was dumped in favour of a common sense chat about future prospects in a life of crime. A twelve-year-old boy with ADHD not currently in school accompanied by a semi-literate, unemployed nineteen-year-old brother will not understand lengthy legal claptrap.

A small number of us were trained in it, and we took it in turn to host the clinic usually during an evening for a couple of hours. It sometimes meant shift changes and typical of most such extra work in the police there wasn't any additional money in it, you did it for the experience.

On 1st April 2007 staff at Fraggle Rock or their partners at the city council, or both working together, decided to rename my beat area and the surrounding beats with a fantastical new title. It was henceforth to be known as the 'Natural Neighbourhood Co-terminus Super Output Area'. I checked the date, but it was real. Someone was being paid a lot of money for this. I imagined the inventors of the title sitting around at home one night listening to Pink Floyd, off their tits on weed, suddenly having a Eureka moment when it popped into their head. It was like a post-war Stalinist five-year plan, more idea than substance. Yet again it was telling us to do something we were already doing.

The beat manager, as my role was now described, worked with a team of PCSOs, the Housing Patch Manager, a special constable and some CPOs. I never had a 'special' working with me, perhaps because I was now too old and grumpy, but more probably because my beat area was deemed to be 'not busy enough'. It wasn't busy because I'd worked damned hard to make it that way. My opinion of special constables was quite low anyway, and I was glad I didn't have one. When I was on response in the '80s and '90s male response drivers were given female specials to be chauffeured around for a few hours in the day-time, but never at night or weekends when it was busy or dangerous. I once attended a domestic incident in Basford when driving a police van full of specials on an evening shift. I remember standing in the tiny living room of the terraced house in Isandula Road when quite suddenly my police radio became incredibly loud. I turned around to see nine specials cramming themselves into the room behind me each with a gormless grin and their radios on full volume. A colleague once remarked that if you told a plumber "Here you are mate, take these people around with you for a day, they know fuck all about plumbing but take them with you anyway," they might not be too impressed. All they can usefully do is watch. I know the Met once spent a fortune on recruiting hundreds of specials and after they all resigned the sum total they had gained after spending millions of pounds amounted to just one person. Policing today is difficult and dangerous, and I don't blame anyone for not wanting to do it, paid or otherwise.

Nottingham now had CPOs working with the police. These were Community Protection Officers, employed by the city council. They also wore police uniforms but had flat caps on their heads like the PCSOs. Only real cops wear helmets, so remember that if you ever want one, though specials can wear them too. The CPOs have a vital role in ensuring the safety of Nottingham's population in that they have to find a minimum number of dog shit offences each month. They are also told to issue tickets for general littering, which includes chucking things out of car windows. Catching people for this is easier than you might think. If a cigarette end or any litter is launched into the street from a car window the CPOs make a note of the registration number and check the vehicle. They have full access to all the police computer systems. I was trained for months on these systems with warnings about data protection and so on, but now these council employees have been given full access. What continues to amaze me is the fact that most people pay these fines of up to £70, when it seems to me there is little or no evidence to prove the offence. There's a story of some CPOs with binoculars sitting in a police station near traffic lights all day looking for littering drivers, but I haven't seen it myself, so I don't know if it's true.

Traffic wardens were disbanded, and parking tickets were taken away from the police. The council set up parking wardens instead. These were yet more people who were allowed to wander about looking like cops. Traffic wardens and cops had been quite used to potential trouble from abusive motorists but the new parking wardens found the great British public a bit of a handful. For years these wardens had to be accompanied by a police officer, particularly at night, to prevent them from being assaulted. So the warden idea was presumably created to save money and yet they needed a cop for protection, usually while being paid overtime. I made quite a bit of money from the scheme so I wasn't complaining.

In the same year I attended Warwick Crown Court to give evidence. Crown Court appearances are relatively rare, particularly for a 'wooden top' as uniformed officers like me were generally known. The CPS won't run anything unless there's at least a 70% chance of success at court, which usually ensures a guilty plea, even if it is at the last minute. There were ten of us cops at court to give evidence against the accused, and it must have cost a fortune. The difference in this case was that the man in the dock was a colleague. He'd been suspended on full pay for *three and a half years,* pending the trial. He'd been accused by the Nottinghamshire Police Professional Standards Department, the PSD, of corruption relating to witnesses and I was there because I'd provided a witness statement. I had been asked if I'd ever seen the officer in possession of blank but signed witness statements. I said no. Had I ever been asked by the officer to obtain signed but blank witness statements? I said no. This was the sum total of my input. I wondered why I'd been called, as it seemed to me that I had no evidence to offer. I swore the oath and gave my evidence in court, dutifully scanning the jury as I did so. In my opinion I hadn't seen the accused doing anything wrong. In the waiting room afterwards I spoke to other colleagues who had a similar story. None of us understood why we were there. It seemed halfway through the day the judge came to the same conclusion and threw it out of court. You have to ask yourself how much the whole sorry mess had cost the taxpayers of Nottingham.

You could find out under a freedom of information request just how many cops in your local force are currently suspended on full pay. Ask them how many lengthy and very costly suspensions resulted in little or no action. Then you could ask for a rate rebate, and see how far you get.

As an award winning cop I was asked to sit on a committee known as the 'On the Streets Working Group'. It was chaired by the deputy chief constable and at the first meeting there were a dozen of us seated around one of the main conference tables at Fraggle Rock. In essence it seemed the gaffers had lost touch with the sharp end and they wanted to canvas opinion. To be fair, most gaffers were promoted off the streets quickly and so it wasn't surprising. I remember a superintendent once made a comment which clearly indicated his distance from the front line by telling a packed briefing room that members of the public had to 'pass the attitude test' in dealings with the police. There was some truth in it of course, but by then it was years since anyone could actually say such a thing aloud.

It was nice to think they might listen to us and we were encouraged to be frank, without fear of reprisal, though none of us believed this second assurance. One of the PCSOs present made a comment about not taking action when faced with a gang of youths in a dark alley, for fear of getting her head kicked in. The deputy chief thought she was joking, and was astonished to think that one of his hard working staff wouldn't risk a damned good kicking and three months in hospital for twenty grand a year. We told him some very awkward home truths and despite warm assurances we would meet regularly there were only a few such meetings before he suddenly became too busy. This was a shame. Those at the top of any huge organisation do lose touch with the workers at the bottom, and to be fair it's understandable, but command with no consultation or knowledge of the sharp end is simply disguised arrogance, because it certainly is not good leadership.

Cannabis factories were springing up everywhere in Nottingham in 2007, and continue to do so today. How the offenders think they can ever hide the smell of five hundred or more mature plants is a mystery. A large town house in the suburb of Sherwood had all its windows covered and was issuing the characteristic sweet smell. We bashed in the front door and charged in. It was like disturbing a hornet's nest. Six oriental males ran from the rear of the property, diving out the windows and doors into the waiting arms of colleagues. I volunteered to stay on and help deal with the arrests. Four of them were called Nguyen, which is the Vietnamese equivalent of Smith, and none of them could speak English. We had to wait six hours for an interpreter to arrive from London, and they all wanted a solicitor, paid for by legal aid of course. Certain drug offences carry the death penalty in Vietnam and so when they were advised that no such fate awaited them other than perhaps three meals a day for a couple of years in a warm furnished cell they began to cooperate.

After initial reticence they eventually told us everything. They had all entered the UK by hiding in a lorry and escaping the vehicle halfway up the A1. At least one of them told us he'd paid the equivalent of £20,000 to get into Britain. I was shocked. Many people would be willing to pay that to get *out* of this country. Every room of the house contained a jungle of tall cannabis plants close to maturity, and there was a formidable system of irrigation and lighting, all run from a dangerous and illegally by-passed electricity meter. It was very slow work interviewing and re-interviewing all six and it took most of the night. We'd started work at 6am and finally finished at 7am the following morning. It was another relatively rare 'good job' coppers enjoy. The Vietnamese lads, who ranged from seventeen to twenty-eight years of age, eventually shared an eleven-year prison sentence. Immigration forms were issued to them at point of charge so when they'd served their time they would be deported. Sadly our inspector wasn't very pleased with us. Despite removing a huge drugs factory from the streets of Nottingham he was clearly thinking of his devolved overtime budget when he said to us: "Don't do this again without asking me, it was only one detection after all." With this comment in mind and the fact that it took him six months to sign through our overtime forms we decided against doing any more.

I joined more committees on my beat area. These included the hospital Trust Security Working Group, and the hospital Trust Security Management Group. I could provide the hospital with detailed, up-to-date crime figures and in return they would ask their teams to improve security at all the crime hotspots. It worked very well and crime continued to fall. When I took over the beat area one of my personal targets was to achieve a crime free weekend at the hospital. Latterly it was common for the entire campus, one of the largest in Europe, to be crime free for a week or even two weeks at a time.

I seemed to attend a lot of meetings. Multi-agency partnership working was seen as the way forward, the 'co-terminus' part of my beat title, and I couldn't escape it. I was a member of several committees which met regularly for child protection, neighbourhood action, youth services and crime prevention. Most of them were worthwhile, but some were clearly not, and for those the Wank Word Bingo sheet came in handy.

In January 2008 I took part in a very dignified rally in London with 27,000 other cops. We were complaining about the government's delay in back-dating a pay rise. On reflection, and taking into account of what the government are currently doing to the police service, this now looks so very trivial. I attended a similar rally twenty years before at Wembley when the Shadow Home Secretary of the day, Tony Blair, assured the gathering of 23,000 cops that the service would be safe in the hands of New Labour. I have to say that these assurances proved largely correct. Cops had until then been mainly Tory supporters, unofficially of course, and they were wary of a Labour government. Margaret Thatcher is now seen to have been the guardian of the police service. I wonder what she would think of the current wholesale dismantling of the British police.

I've witnessed the same in the NHS too, when working

at the hospital. It seems everything is being privatised, from catering to cleaning. Local people who've worked in the health service for generations now find themselves working for private companies on lower rates of pay, changed working conditions, and little or no pension. As in any such organisation complaints are met with the usual comments of 'If you don't like it, the door's there.' The changes in the health service are implemented using a climate of fear specifically created to ensure what's really happening is not leaked to the public or the media.

In 2009 we were issued with Blackberry phones. They were linked to some of the force computer systems and we would eventually use them to input crime and other incidents directly into the new crime database. The CRIS system had gone, thankfully. The keys on a Blackberry were tiny, as you might know. Learning to input complex information using the QWERTY keyboard on the phone was difficult at first. We were encouraged to use the hand-held device, as it was euphemistically known, instead of calling the control room, as it was all part of the government's £7m drive for the police to use 'mobile data'. If the idea was to get cops back out on the streets to be more visible then it was another dismal failure. The discipline had long since gone and some cops continued to spend entire shifts in the station sitting at a computer looking very busy but actually doing nothing.

Anti-social behaviour, or kids messing about, continued to be a problem on other people's beat areas. It was decided to use beat managers such as myself to staff a patrol car specifically to deal with ASB. This became known as Operation Cacogen, and still runs to this day. It was quickly known by its practitioners as Operation Cack Again. It was unpopular because of course ASB only usually happens in the evenings, and mainly on Friday and Saturday nights. Consequently day shifts were changed, rest days cancelled, and time off refused, all in the service of the Cack Again monster. Driving around the city knocking stuff on the head in this manner is soul destroying and pointless, but the gaffers seem to love it.

For more than twenty-five years I was known by one radio call sign, my collar number, 512. By 2011 I had acquired a total of four. When working on Cack Again and similar operations I was not only 512, but also CB822, LB35, or CASB01, depending on the role I was undertaking. Bearing in mind your ear becomes attuned to your call sign so you can hear it almost instinctively over all other noises, to be called different things on different days was ludicrous. The reason for it of course, was simply in order to suit the command and control database being used at Fraggle Rock. The dog was yet again thoroughly wagged by the tail.

Cack Again was city wide. You could therefore find yourself at the far end of the city in a strange area, usually at night, talking to kids you'd never met before and who you were unlikely to ever meet again, trying to build a relationship and an understanding with them in five minutes flat. It simply doesn't work. You might say cops should just turn up and tell the kids off and do as they are told, and some cops do conduct themselves in this manner, but the kids just look at you, think that you are a complete twat, and carry on as soon as you've gone. ASB callers would come out of their houses and reveal the offender to be the lad down the road, you know the one, he always wears a blue top, and he ran up the jitty as usual, just there, you know the one... well; actually I don't, because I've never been here before. The question asked by astonished members of the public when I told them I usually worked at the hospital five miles away was: “What are you doing here?” But as usual the gaffers loved Cack Again because someone, anyone, was addressing a problem the gaffers above them – the other monkeys in the tree – had asked them to find a solution to. In my humble opinion the service to the public was embarrassingly shoddy and unprofessional.

THE END

THE FALL AND RISE

By 2012 large cracks began appearing in the police service. These were mainly gaps in staffing levels and shortages of vehicles. As usual the gaffers were desperate to do something about it so some of the extraneous squads were reduced or disbanded. Nottinghamshire lost the mounted section and the OSU, Operational Support Unit, was cut. The OSU, or 'the unit' as it was known, were based in the woods at Fraggle Rock and were a team of mainly male officers who were used to police football matches, special events and so on. They have been variously known as the Force Support Unit and the Special Operations Unit, but such names apparently sounded too aggressive for the Labour city council. Their numbers have now dwindled to such an extent that other cops have to stand in and do the jobs they used to do. There's an obvious irony and clear stupidity in reducing a team in favour of saving jobs at the front line when by doing so their job then has to be done by cops from the front line. This happens a lot in the police service, and no doubt across the entire public sector. It's like rearranging the deck chairs again, and sadly it's getting worse.

In 1968 Nottinghamshire County Police and Nottingham City Police amalgamated into Nottinghamshire Constabulary, and four divisions, A, B, C, and D were created. There was always a running joke among those at the sharp end that at times of crisis the gaffers would decide to change it back to City and County. In 2011 the four divisions disappeared and Nottinghamshire Police was indeed split into City Division and County Division. It seems yet again that going backwards is the way forward.

In the last few years of my service I was frequently removed from my normal duties to police various events across the city, problems that until then were usually addressed by the OSU. Operation Country takes place on the coldest and wettest October nights every year, and runs alongside Operation Graduate. The purpose of Op Country is to bring down the high number of burglaries and street crime in a certain area and Op Graduate is to provide reassurance to the 60,000 ungrateful middle-class piss-heads masquerading as students who come to live in the worst parts of the city. These always follow the annual fun of Goose Fair. All three involve trudging the streets wearing a big hat in an entirely pointless manner getting soaked and very tired.

I turned up at Canning Circus police station in the city centre one Saturday afternoon to work from 5pm until 1am on Operation Graduate. I had already been changed from a day shift so when I arrived for work I should have been at home. At 6pm we were told we would be kept on duty until 6am. It rained all night. The modern police uniform can best be described as utterly shit. It couldn't keep the wearer dry in a desert. The reflective yellow jacket stops at the waist and is not waterproof. The rain runs down onto your legs and in ten minutes you are wet through to the skin. You then have to walk around in more rain for ten hours in this condition.

My biggest problem with being frequently abstracted was that back in the real world, at the hospital or on the housing estates of my own beat area, jobs began piling up. I could read about the incidents on the computer from a distance and there were many occasions where I knew who an offender was and could have dealt with the matter quickly and informally but I was miles away and not due back for weeks. I repeatedly pointed this out but I was told by sergeants and inspectors not to worry about it. Abstractions were something we would just have to get used to; but I began to lose touch with my beat area and, worse still, the music club began to collapse because of my frequent evening commitments elsewhere. I protested but was told to get on with my work; my beat area was not my concern when I was away from it. I always found this statement rather peculiar because when back on our beat areas we were given weekly statistics of crime and ASB trends with concerned questions as to why certain crimes had risen. When I stated the reason may be because I hadn't been on my beat area for a while I was told: "That's got nothing to do with it."

Even when I wasn't abstracted a gaffer told me I was only allowed two hours a week for the music club, saying: "You're a police officer, not a youth worker." For the first time in years ASB began to rise across my beat. At first I felt personally affronted by this, but as the abstractions continued, and I was again told not to worry about it, I did just that. I gave up. If the people above me in the rank structure displayed a total lack of concern then why should I bother? This is a perfect example of utterly uninspiring leadership.

Crime began falling in 2002. From the peak in the mid-90s total crime in England and Wales in 2012 was around 9.5 million and has continued a sharp downward trend, though with some fluctuations at times. The national homicide rate dropped to 550 in 2012, exactly the same as in 1983. Harold Shipman, the murdering doctor, apparently killed 215 people so he briefly skewed the figures a little. You might wonder what the police are doing if crime rates are falling so much, but the crime figures have been boosted by some new recording trends which take up huge amounts of time. In the twelve months to July 2014 Nottinghamshire Police recorded 33,541 incidents of ASB, anti-social behaviour. Total crime was 105,343 for the same year, so according to these figures they spent a third of their time dealing with kids making nuisances of themselves.

You won't believe how much time is consumed by ASB these days. Each incident of ASB generates a crime number. It's not a crime as such, even though the procedures are the same, and a cop spends forty-five minutes on his or her Blackberry trying to generate one. It's known as a non-crime ASB crime number. There's nowhere else to record them so they are entered onto the crime database. This then means a four-page crime report must be completed, and then a written risk assessment. The victim has to be visited and contacted regularly on a specific schedule which must be strictly observed, for ever. There's no end date to the revisits if the problem persists. If you work for the Home Office or you are currently a gaffer I can hear you agreeing with this, and it does sound great, but it's a logistical nightmare. I had very many victims of ASB telling me after my tenth visit not to bother them any more as they were fed up of the police calling round to the house every other day.

The same also applies to cases of domestic violence. Quite right too, I hear you say, and I agree to a certain extent. Years ago the police were not interested in domestic violence. We'd just take the offender, usually the male partner, to his mother's house for the night, leaving the female at the address crying into the kitchen sink. But one of the last jobs I dealt with was one brother verbally bullying another in the same household. I was tasked to visit the brothers every week for the rest of their lives. Presumably now that I've retired someone else will be paying them regular visits. If one of the brothers told me he had been shouted at again by the other I then had to generate an entirely new non-crime domestic crime number, fill in the four-page crime report, and then another two-page written risk assessment, and again if he did it the following week, and so on, forever. I'm not joking. If you wondered why you never see a police officer these days you now know why.

I submitted a report – which as usual was ignored – suggesting we deal with wind damage in the same protracted manner, merely for the sake of recording it because nobody else did. A fence blown down in a storm could be a non-crime wind-related crime number, generating a wind-related non-crime crime report and risk assessment, at least a couple of hour's police time utterly wasted. Why not? The police could even sell the statistics to insurance companies, generate some revenue, target repeat wind victims, and assist in the long term rectification of the problem, i.e., buy a new fence. We need not stop there. A dead bird in the street could become a non-crime dead-bird related crime number, and the figures could be used by the RSPB or RSPCA to monitor wildlife levels, because nobody else is doing it. Recently, the *Thunderbirds* puppet known as Tom Winsor in his role as HMIC stated that police use of discretion had prevented thousands of crimes from being recorded. So, let's do as he asks and record everything we see!

I'm not saying the police shouldn't take matters of ASB and domestic violence seriously, but in 2014 there has to be a more efficient way of doing it. If and when crime starts rising again there simply won't be sufficient time available. The service to the victim in my opinion is overly attentive to the point of being almost pressured, and the reasons for it are very definitely not purely to provide a good service. The main reason for such procedures, as everyone knows who works in the public sector, is as an insurance policy. It is common knowledge that most of what cops do today is covering their back in case something goes wrong. It sometimes seemed as though more time was spent doing this than actually doing the job. If someone is found dead the first thing that is looked for is blame. I don't mean who the offender was, but which public servant didn't do their job properly. The media seem to concentrate all their efforts on finding out who they can publicly hang while the real offender and victim are often side-lined as irrelevant. Minor mistakes and accidents happen. No-one can provide gilt-edged guarantees against the random behaviour of human beings; it's what makes us human, so get over it.

In 2010 I started sending stroppy letters to the police magazine *Police Review*, mainly about how shit the job was becoming. They must have thought I was Mr Angry, but to their credit they published quite a few. Eventually they became so pissed off by my frequent ranting that they offered me a regular column. I was paid the glorious sum of £70 for five hundred words every month. I was thrilled. Suddenly I was a professional writer and had fulfilled a lifelong dream. I obtained formal permission to be a columnist from my employers in the form of a 'Business Interest' and thoroughly enjoyed the experience. Most of my ramblings were directed at the crazy policies oozing from the arse-end of the Home Office, as was most of the magazine's content. It was no surprise such dissent was stifled when the publication ceased in 2012 despite being profitable. It was probably in preparation for the oncoming slaughter of the service that has taken place since.

My column in *Police Review* inspired me to write further, so I began collecting some of the incidents I'd dealt with at the hospital. Friends in the pub couldn't believe I'd dealt with a doctor who regularly masturbated at nurses in his coffee breaks, and another who stole a huge television, so there was a clear interest in the subject. During Op Graduate in October 2010 I wandered alone through the dark streets of Nottingham all night in the rain while during the day I'd write. The following year I published my first book, *Hospital Beat,* about my antics at the Nottingham City Hospital. It was an immediate success. The initial print run of a thousand paperback copies sold out quickly, despite the fact that I had to classify it as fiction, when a huge amount of it was factual.

In 2011, while again trudging the streets of Canning Circus in the rain every night for two months, I began writing my second book, *Kibbutz Virgin.* One morning in November 2011 I almost collapsed at home feeling dizzy and unwell. My doctor sent me to hospital and, to my astonishment, after a scan I was informed I had a blood clot, an embolism, on my right lung. 30% of people who acquire such things die in their sleep. I was told I would be off work

RUBBER HEALS AND RESENTMENT

I had twenty-eight years unblemished service. I'd never hit anyone, I'd never used my CS spray and I'd never had a complaint upheld against me. That's not to say I'd never been in receipt of complaints. Many people complain about police officers, and it's usually at the point of arrest because they don't like being caught. In today's society where parents and teachers are reluctant to use force it comes as a shock when handcuffs are applied.

I was proud of a clear discipline record, and I considered myself to be a good cop. I'd never been interviewed by the Complaints and Discipline Department as they were once known. They were also known as the 'rubber heal brigade' because they could easily sneak up on the unwary. Such things happened frequently to other cops, but not to me, and so I was shocked when the Professional Standards Department, the PSD, came for me on 1st March 2012.

I was served discipline notices for my book *Hospital Beat.* There were thirteen parts of it that were apparently 'unacceptable'. Not only this, I was informed I didn't have permission to publish it. I was stunned. My writing had become incredibly important to me and I loved it with a passion. I was close to retirement and it would soon become my second career. I immediately argued that I had been given permission to write as a columnist, but I was told 'columnist' is different to 'writer'. At first I thought someone was joking. I assured them that the book had been classified as fiction, but this didn't seem to have any impact. I also reminded them that Nottinghamshire Police, or even the word 'Nottingham', never appeared in the book. The wording of the charge was:

Jonathan Nicholas describes actions, attitudes and opinions that, if true, would result in disciplinary action and which in any case bring Nottinghamshire Police into disrepute.

The book was classified as fiction, and Nottingham isn't mentioned, so how could this be possible? My Business Interest as a columnist was variously described in different articles of paperwork from the PSD as 'Freelance Journalist' and 'Freelance columnist' which they corrected months later to 'Police Review Columnist', and in the notices served on me the investigator referred to it as 'Writer'. Were they just incompetent or merely confused? In the wording of the Business Interest it says 'You should not appear in uniform' and yet my monthly *Police Review* article carried a photo of me in my uniform, but this was never mentioned. Was it selective discipline?

The whole matter started when a member of staff at Fraggle Rock decided he didn't like the book. He stated some of the contents were 'as bad if not worse than the recent Channel 4 *Coppers* TV programme' where Nottinghamshire officers frequently described members of the public as 'snaffs'. There isn't a single mention of that word in the entire book, and besides, as I kept reminding them, it was classed as fiction. In the discipline paperwork this person found the book 'personally unacceptable'. He wasn't the chief constable, he wasn't even a high ranking police officer, nor was he in the PSD, so who was he to make this judgement on a *personal* basis? Presumably had he liked it nothing would have happened? This appeared to me to be a bizarre and astonishingly unprofessional way of conducting discipline issues.

All that summer I had battles with the PSD. I was interviewed for two hours under caution and on tape like a criminal. My interviewer was a retired cop himself who'd been working as a civvie in the PSD for ten years. Why someone would want to do this I have no idea. Cops have no real need to work again after retirement, particularly if a partner continues to work, but I suppose greed can be a powerful motivator.

Eventually, seven months later, I attended a 'Misconduct Meeting' at Fraggle Rock. I had a brilliant Police Federation representative with me, and the meeting was chaired by a gaffer I'd never met before. Even though it was supposed to be a meeting to discuss the issues I had a feeling the outcome was predestined. The expression 'kangaroo court' springs to mind. I was found guilty of bringing the police service into disrepute, and publishing a book without permission. I was shocked. I was also bemused that my employers apparently considered themselves reputational guardians of the entire police service, and not just themselves. I wondered if the other forty-two forces in England and Wales were appreciative of their efforts to quash the publication of such a damaging book.

I had been in direct email contact with the chief constable about the book and she didn't seem to have an issue with it. She even asked me if it was available in Kindle format. Clearly it seemed to me that some discipline issues were being dictated purely on a personal basis by a single employee with an apparent dislike of certain books.

I was told I'd brought discredit on the police service by

publishing an outrageous book without permission. I'd been left hanging for seven months, and exchanged dozens of emails with the PSD and the Federation. My defence case was a folder an inch thick, as was the prosecution case compiled by the PSD. Many hours of work and a huge amount of police time had been spent on both sides, and it must have cost a small fortune. The matter had been foremost in my mind and I was very worried about it, as was my wife. *Kibbutz Virgin* was ready to publish, but my writing was on hold because I was told I couldn't publish anything while the case was pending. I awaited my punishment.

There were thirteen parts of the book that were deemed unacceptable, and these are as follows:

1. The chapter 'EAU' where I described in my own thoughts that a nurse's legs were rather nice. I was told: 'We don't want the public to think serving police officers have such thoughts'.
2. The chapter 'Bobby' where I described in my own thoughts my opinion of a particular career criminal as 'a scruffy, thieving, pernicious little bastard'.
3. The same chapter when I described the same man in the book as 'a cockroach'.
4. The same chapter where I described levels of acceptable dishonesty amongst the public.
5. The chapter 'Coffee' where I disposed of a suspect package without calling the bomb squad, risking my life but breaching protocol.
6. The chapter 'Logistics' where the words 'cunt' and 'twat' are used privately between me and a colleague. 'We don't want the public to think police officers use that kind of language'.

7. The chapter 'Jimmy' where in my own thoughts I described a violent criminal as 'a thin and scruffy bastard'.
8. The same chapter where I shouted at a violent criminal in the police van who had been threatening doctors and nurses, calling him 'an arrogant fucking shit'.
9. The chapter 'Race'. They didn't like this. You will have to read it.
10. The chapter 'Maternity', where I described a member of the great British underclass having a baby and stealing from everyone else on the ward.
11. The same chapter where I described a female criminal's persistent use of the word 'fuck'.
12. The same chapter where I charged the woman while she was actually giving birth.
13. The chapter 'Lies' where I described a previous colleague ogling the hospital's nurses.

It seemed to me that the list had been drawn up by Oliver Cromwell or some other Puritan. I was astonished, more so when I knew of other police books written by serving officers from other forces that were similar, but their employers had no problem with them. Clearly they didn't allow personal opinions by minor members of staff to dictate discipline policy. Other serving cops had their photographs on Amazon claiming their books were true. I had done neither. It seemed it was all down to a personal dislike of the book, and probably me. I wondered for a while if it was thought that I was Jewish and these actions were prompted by anti-Semitism, but I couldn't prove it.

I was astonished when the decision on the matter finally came. I was to receive 'No action'. Not even advice or a telling off. The gaffer who chaired the discipline meeting later told me what he thought of the case, the PSD and me. He was very sympathetic but is still a serving officer so I cannot write about it. Gaffers are dragged from across the force to chair these disciplinary meetings and generally do not work in the PSD themselves. After it was concluded I wondered just how much the whole thing had cost the taxpayer, and for no result.

I applied for permission to publish *Kibbutz Virgin,* but this was refused by PSD. It seemed they really didn't like me by this time. I'd escaped them once and it seemed they wouldn't let go. I appealed directly to the assistant chief constable and it was upheld when he bypassed the PSD. I could publish the story about my exploits in Israel in 1978 provided it didn't include anything of Nottinghamshire Police. Not a chance. The book was finally released to the world six months late. I was then forced to withdraw *Hospital Beat* from worldwide sale, due to its scurrilous content. Amazon told me they had never known an author remove a book from sale in this manner, and it took a month. It was re-released eighteen months later when I retired, but by then it had lost some momentum, which it took time to regain. Meanwhile I was told my face could not be displayed on social media, Amazon or any other public arena, and so I was unable to hold book launches or publicity of any sort, all the usual things that authors undertake.

During the process of being banned from publishing I felt strangely impotent, censored like a Cold War Eastern European poet. It was an odd feeling, and very unnerving, like being the subject of a police fatwa. I hated it.

In December 2012 the PSD came for me again. I was

served discipline notices for putting a poor review of a book on Amazon under an anonymous female pseudonym. I wondered at first if the same person at Fraggle Rock was behind it. I wasn't abusive or insulting in any way, I just said the book was dreadful. It seemed the writer of the book found out from his own research that I was a serving police officer and had complained to Nottinghamshire Police that the review wasn't good enough. As a private individual surely I was allowed to write book reviews on Amazon? I'd written dozens and I suddenly thought about my favourite authors such as Anthony Beevor, Dirk Bogarde, Emily Bronte, Boris Pasternak and Christopher Hitchens. I knew most of them were dead but would someone make complaints about these reviews too? I wasn't disclosing my occupation; the man had to conduct some extensive enquiries to trace me. I'd used a female pseudonym on the review specifically in order to disguise myself. Ironically, even though they had stated they wanted to protect the reputation of Nottinghamshire Police I was told it was they who informed the man that Jonathan Nicholas was one of their officers. I thought this was bizarre and I have no idea why they did it.

Nottinghamshire Police took the complaint, Case Reference CO/00418/12. I was astonished. If I thought there wasn't a personal vendetta against me before, then surely there was now? Just because you are paranoid doesn't mean they are not out to get you of course. I was served a Regulation 15 Police (Complaints & Misconduct) Regulations 2012(Subject) Notice. The offence was 'Multiple or Unspecified breaches of PACE'. I was dumbfounded and awaited my fate with interest. How on earth had I breached the Police and Criminal Evidence Act 1984, and on multiple occasions?

Weeks later I was informed the matter of the poor Amazon review would not be taken any further. No explanation was given, and no apology forthcoming. As a result of this my paranoia increased. It seemed to me that I was being unfairly scrutinised. I've read about life in occupied Europe during World War Two, and the secret to survival was avoiding coming to the notice of the Gestapo, because once they knew of you then it seemed they would never let go.

I was then moved to a police station four miles away from my beat area, for no logical reason. It was certainly not, in my opinion, for any operational purpose; it made my job much harder. I protested because it didn't make any sense but was told bluntly to get on with my work, the matter was not up for discussion. I could catch a bus to my beat area during office hours but there was no direct route after 6pm and at weekends. Instead of being literally right at the edge of my beat it would now take me an hour to get there.

In May 2013 the PSD struck again. They'd discovered something form 2010 and served me discipline notices. I was accused of not properly investigating and recording the disclosure of sexual abuse. This seems laughable now, when so many British police forces covered up such things on a wholesale basis. The complaint hadn't even come from a member of the public but from a colleague, a person in the sexual offences unit, probably using the new 'Grass on a colleague hotline'.

In 2010 I dealt with a particularly obnoxious man for criminal damage to his father's car. In interview I allowed him to tell me on tape for ten minutes that it was nothing to do with him, he was nowhere near the car that night, and that I was just picking on him because I didn't like him. I then played him the very clear CCTV showing him committing the offence, including all his threats and abusive language, on some very good audio. His face dropped and he went very quiet. He then started blubbering, mumbling about his father. He made references to sexual abuse and being 'shagged by him' when he was young, which I admit I didn't believe. The man was an inveterate liar and couldn't lie straight in bed. Villains will often invent mitigation, excuses for their behaviour, and I was sure this was one of those occasions.

I played along with him, as you do, in order to get the cough on tape. I then asked him about the allegations of abuse and several times told him we should go upstairs after the interview to the sexual abuse unit to sort it out. The 'shag your own kids department' as we called it was in the same building, so his problem could be resolved very quickly. Each time I made this suggestion he didn't give a direct reply. I knew then that it was nonsense. I'd recently assisted social services in removing some of his children into foster care because of his negligent parenting, so I'm pretty sure he didn't like me very much. I didn't like him, but I didn't hate him. After the interview he was charged and bailed to court. He couldn't get out the police station fast enough. He didn't ask about going upstairs or reporting anything else. This was further indication to me that it was complete crap.

In the light of the Jimmy Saville revelations, unknown to me the man had attended the police station to report the matter early in 2013. You can only guess his motivation. The sex squad emailed me asking about it because he'd mentioned my name. Astonishingly the man had told them he'd reported it to me in 2010 adding in a very accusatory manner "but he did nothing about it." I assured them that the abuse allegation against his father was nonsense, but they informed the PSD, hence the discipline notices. They must have been delighted when it arrived in their office with my name on it.

If you are a long-retired cop you might remember the 'complaints and discipline' department being fairly sympathetic to police officers who were facing mischievous allegations from dishonest criminals with long records. Common sense often played a role in such matters and whether you agree or not, cops were often given the benefit of the doubt. It was acknowledged that being a cop was a difficult and stressful job, and it was common for criminals to make malicious complaints. But it seems if a complaint is made today there is an immediate presumption of guilt. Cops are no longer trusted to be as truthful as they once were. It's now almost impossible to get a criminal convicted merely on the word of one police officer. I suppose the police service has brought this upon itself to a certain extent, with the Guildford Four, Hillsborough and so on. But don't forget these highly public miscarriages of justice and apparent cover-ups were managed by gaffers, and the cops on the ground were acting on their instructions. Standing up and questioning orders can be extremely difficult in any organisation, but particularly so in the police.

After six weeks the matter was mysteriously upgraded to gross misconduct and I was threatened with dismissal. I was only a few months away from retirement. The point of issue was that I had not taken the man's complaint seriously, and had not acted on it. I reminded the PSD that I had offered the man help no less than four times during the interview, and it was recorded on the tape transcript, but this was seemingly not good enough. Suddenly I remembered I had an independent witness who heard me offer the man assistance, and the man's subsequent refusal of my help. I contacted the lady in a partner agency and she remembered it clearly. With a huge sense of relief I immediately emailed her details to the PSD.

Weeks passed but my independent witness told me she had not yet been contacted. She was a crucial witness, so how could this be? In desperation I emailed the investigating officer in the PSD and informed him of my intention to submit a formal grievance that he wasn't investigating the case properly. You can imagine the impact of this. I felt vindicated when less than an hour later my independent witness informed me the PSD wanted to see her. It seemed I was driving my own investigation into myself.

The discipline issue hung over me constantly like a dark cloud. I made enquiries with the Police Federation and the PSD again informed me that I could be dismissed. I'd lose my pension and all the plans I had for my wife and family I'd nurtured for years were suddenly in jeopardy. We looked at our finances and if I lost everything it seemed we'd have to sell the family home immediately and downsize. My family and I were devastated.

While all this was happening I still had to work. My mind wandered and with the real prospect of losing everything I began to descend into dark despair. On two occasions for an instant I thought about the consequences of stepping into traffic, in uniform, on the busy Nottingham ring road. The main reason I didn't was thoughts of my family and also how unfair it would be on the drivers. I had problems from another source while at work. A sergeant would frequently call me up when at the hospital telling me to return to the station to see him 'for ten minutes'. When

I told him where I was he was still insistent. This same sergeant kept telling me I couldn't cope and I was at risk of losing my job through incompetence. Stress causes poor decision making and absentmindedness, which in turn causes more stress, and so it goes on. How could I have descended from being the best cop in the force only a few years before to getting the sack for being crap? I didn't understand what was going on.

For years when on early shifts I'd sit at a computer eating my cereal while checking what had happened overnight on my beat area. No-one ever minded, and it only took five minutes. There were just a few of us who did it anyway, and only on the early shifts, which were not particularly frequent. Suddenly there was a blanket ban on eating in work time, other than for the statutory forty-five minutes at lunchtime. The female gaffer said: "I don't want to see anyone eating at their desks in the morning." In my state of paranoia I believed this was directed at me. I knew I'd be safe in the gents' locker room so for the rest of my service I ate my Weetabix standing up in the gent's toilet. After several months I became accustomed to eating breakfast with the heady whiff of urinals, Lynx deodorant and semi-naked men with their knobs hanging out.

I've noticed one of the new ways discipline has been attempted in the police service latterly is the catch-all bollocking. If a member of staff is repeatedly late or dares to eat Weetabix at their desk then a widespread ban on such practices is issued. It means that everyone is told not to do something that most were not doing in the first place. In my opinion this is the worst kind of David Brent style of leadership and causes huge resentment amongst those who are not involved.

I've suffered migraines all my life but when happy and healthy I would only get one or two a year. I began to get two or three a week, and I dreaded a bad one at work, but it was becoming inevitable. I was in full uniform on one occasion in Sherwood high street talking to a member of the public when I suddenly realised I'd lost sight of his face. This is called prosopagnosia and I only usually get this during the onset of a severe attack. It effectively means having to wait for someone to speak so you can tell who it is. It's a prelude to pain. With all these negative circumstances coming together I began to lose my self-confidence, which can cause major problems for a front-line cop.

Finally in August I received the 'disclosure documents' from the PSD. The documents stated the matter was merely misconduct and not gross misconduct. I queried this and was told it was still gross misconduct. They sent me the correct form a few days later. The disclosure documents were intended for the accused to see the nature and strength of the evidence. Of the eight items listed I was given sight of only three. Criminals are treated more fairly.

The summary made by the investigator in my opinion was poor and evidentially inaccurate in many places. I complained and submitted a mitigation statement detailing the inaccuracies. This was ignored. I was visited by the line manager of the PSD investigator who was the subject of my grievance complaint. I wasn't surprised to hear my grievance against him was going nowhere. It seemed the PSD investigated themselves and came to the conclusion they had no case to answer.

I know a colleague who was investigated for over two years and was charged with computer misuse. Like so many others he was suspended on full pay. He was charged and bailed to Crown Court. A possible prison sentence was looming. You can imagine the prospects of a decent family man, and a cop, going to prison. Three days before the trial it was decided there wasn't enough evidence to pursue the matter. His barrister had been saying the same thing all along. He was reinstated as a cop but even though he had many years in the job he decided to leave. He'd been through years of hell for nothing, and who could say it might not happen again? He told me he couldn't trust his employers any longer. This displays an astonishing lack of faith in the integrity of a police force but is not an isolated case. I know at least one other cop who has actually moved house into a neighbouring county because they don't trust their own police. During the investigation into my friend's case the interview transcript notes were found unattended in an insecure office of a police station. They had apparently been left there by the PSD investigator, who had forgotten them. The notes were of evidential value and more importantly were highly confidential. This was a serious breach of protocol. My colleague complained to the PSD and he was assured the matter was 'extremely serious and would be thoroughly investigated'. I was told the PSD officer responsible was given 'advice' and the matter quickly concluded, with no suspension for months or years, no disciplinary hearing, nothing.

In August 2010 a high ranking Nottinghamshire officer appeared on the front page of the local newspaper, openly criticising the accuracy of the speed camera equipment used by Nottinghamshire Police after being caught driving at 79mph in a 50mph limit. Such public criticism clearly brought the force into serious disrepute. There was potential for hundreds or thousands of others to raise the same issue. You can imagine the consequences if I'd done the same. Eventually a guilty plea was offered, after dragging the force very publicly through the mud. As far as I know nothing ever happened about it. Why was this not worse than publishing a book about an anonymous hospital?

In my opinion if you have persons in authority who become so arrogant that they believe they are above the law, then you create a potentially dangerous situation. This is further exacerbated if these persons are cops.

With only five months left of my service and the PSD informing again that I could be dismissed I couldn't take the pressure any longer. I was signed off work with stress. Finally in October 2013 I was summoned to Fraggle Rock for interview with the PSD. For the first time I met the muppet I'd been having email conversations with for months. He looked very nervous and not once did he make eye contact with me. The other man was his line manager, the person I'd met before when my grievance was thrown in the bin. He was typical of the sort and I know he believed himself to be above walking a beat in uniform because he'd said as much to a colleague years before. Why do people join the police in order not to be cops?

I had a wonderful representative from the Police Federation who was quick to point out the important issues. The two PSD muppets reminded me of Zippy and Bungle from the children's TV series *Rainbow*, and one of the first things I made sure was included on the tape was a mistake the investigator had made. The matter had yet again been classed incorrectly on the form I had been served.

"Did you write this form?" I asked, as I held it up for Zippy to see.

"Yes I did," he replied.

"Is it gross misconduct or misconduct?"

"Oh, right, yes, my mistake," he said, looking at the form, as he fumbled about and handed me a correct one.

"We are allowed to make mistakes then?" I asked, as his face flushed but he didn't reply.

I listened to them ranting at me as though I was in a dream, or a nightmare. They began criticising my interviewing skills during the 2010 investigation, both firing questions at me as though I was one of the Great Train Robbers. My federation representative interjected with:

"Is this officer under investigation for an additional matter of negligent interviewing? If so are you going to charge him with anything else?"

"Er… no."

"Then is it relevant to this case?"

"Er… no."

It seems that in 2010 when the man first raised the issue of abuse I should have completed a crime report about it. The fact the man was reluctant to do so and indeed didn't seem to want to talk to me was apparently irrelevant. I should have completed a crime report with few, if any, details just as long as I had made the report. It all seemed too ludicrous. I was probably going to lose my job and everything I'd worked for because I hadn't submitted a blank form nearly four years before. I always thought headquarters was an insane asylum full of mad people, hence the nickname Fraggle Rock, but now I was convinced. I had insisted all along that this was a 'learning and development' issue and not a discipline issue. I wasn't aware of the value placed on blank forms.

The interview ran into a second forty-five minute tape. I was reminded at the start that I was under caution. I nodded and shook my head and let my federation representative do most of the talking. At the end when I left the room I did so without speaking to the two muppets and I didn't shake their hands. In all my life I've never before encountered such depths of personal animosity. I know a serving officer who has had problems from the PSD who told me if he ever saw certain members of the department walking by a road he wouldn't hesitate in running them over and killing them. I don't feel as bad as that but I can fully understand the hatred.

Christmas came while I was still off sick. On 27th January 2014 I was summoned to the police station. I was served a 'Performance Record' form in which I was told the matter was indeed a 'learning and development' issue and not a discipline matter, as I had been saying all along. The PSD had decided it was again merely misconduct and a local gaffer could give me 'verbal advice' about it. This was only one step up from no action at all. There had probably been hundreds of hours of police time spent on this matter, again for nothing. There was a huge amount of paperwork generated on both sides; increasingly precious police time spent trying to discipline me instead of preventing and detecting crime.

I was told that in future I was to deal with such disclosures using the correct procedures and if I had any doubts I should seek advice. I was three weeks away from retirement. The matter had been misconduct, then gross misconduct, then misconduct and then gross misconduct again, then finally misconduct. It's ironic that a department that claims the title Professional Standards, in my opinion, seems to me to be distinctly lacking in both professionalism and standards.

I have since been informed that my hunch regarding the man's sexual abuse claim was correct, and it was found to be unsubstantiated. Complete bollocks, in other words.

While I was off work in the last few months of my service I was in email contact with several members of the public on my beat area. Very few knew the real reasons why I'd not been at work. They said they were missing me, and in turn I missed several good jobs at the hospital. The saddest part was that the music club collapsed.

I retired at midnight on 19th February 2014. I opened a bottle of champagne but I was still very much in a dark place. What Churchill described as his 'black dog' was with me all the time.

I'd been to dozens of happy retirement parties over the years with gifts and speeches and amusing anecdotes. I ended my thirty years with no ceremony, no handshake, no party, nothing. I just didn't go there anymore.

EPILOGUE

My advice to anyone thinking of joining the police now is please don't, it's dreadful. Once you step outside the doors of the police station you are on your own. It seems nowadays that almost any mistake can get you into trouble, sacked or even imprisoned.

I know many serving cops now who tell me that when at work they do as little as possible, not because they are idle, and I know they are not, but because the less they do, the less chance there is of falling foul of the Draconian discipline system.

The contrast between being inside a job, and in particular a modern, politically correct machine such as the police service, and being outside it, is now huge. When on the inside you live in a bizarre gentile world like that of the *Eloi* in HG Wells' The Time Machine, where no-one upsets anyone and all humanity is wonderful. Nasty and uncomfortable things are avoided but if they do occur they are hidden, as though they didn't actually happen, because no-one wants to upset anyone. That's why it's easier for public bodies nowadays to ignore awkward problems rather than actually confront them.

It's ironic that the concept of political correctness was probably created like all religions in a dream in order to protect vulnerable members of society. What has actually happened is that it has allowed dreadful things to happen, and I cannot see this situation improving.

Anyone standing up and pointing out that such horrible things might really be happening, or indeed anyone who dares to speak out against the flow is quickly silenced. When you live inside the bubble it's not obvious, but after escaping it all seems very clear.

I spoke to many people who are inside other public sector organisations in Britain today and all dissent is crushed. I've no doubt that one day very soon the government will introduce a law banning anyone from revealing anything about life in the police, prisons, the NHS, teaching, and so on, even after retirement. Eventually no-one will know what the hell is going on. This is presumably just how the government wants it to be.

Where's Winston Smith when you need him?

ACKNOWLEDGEMENTS

My usual thanks to Jeremy Thompson and his fantastic team at Troubador; we never stop learning! Thank you to colleagues both serving and no longer in the police, NHS, and prison service for snippets of memory, anecdotes and information. Many of my colleagues are still serving, and so I had to be very careful not to identify them, I wouldn't want the Thought Police Nazis kicking in their front door at 6am one day. Sadly the laws of slander and libel prevented me from naming some of the idiots in this book. If they read this they might realise who I'm talking about, but you won't.

Nineteen Eighty-Four by George Orwell (Copyright George Orwell, 1948), reprinted by permission of Bill Hamilton as the Literary Executor of the Estate of the Late Sonia Brownell Orwell.

My biggest thank you is to my wife, for her support through three decades and in particular the last few horrendous years. Thank you.

שוקולד